KT-440-346

COOK ESPAÑA,

A CULINARY JOURNEY AROUND THE FOOD AND DRINK OF SPAIN

DRINK ESPAÑA!

COOK ESPAÑA, DRINK ESPAÑA!

A CULINARY JOURNEY AROUND THE FOOD AND DRINK OF SPAIN

JOHN RADFORD & MARIO SANDOVAL

PHOTOGRAPHY BY JEAN-BLAISE HALL

MITCHELL BEAZLEY

NORWICH CITY COLLEGE

Stock No	246528	
Class	641.5946 RAD	
Cat.		Proc 3WL

Cook España, Drink España!
John Radford and Mario Sandoval

First published in Great Britain in 2007 by Mitchell Beazley,
an imprint of Octopus Publishing Group Limited,
2–4 Heron Quays, London E14 4JP.
An Hachette Livre UK Company
www.octopusbooks.co.uk

Copyright © Octopus Publishing Group Limited 2007
Text © John Radford and Mario Sandoval 2007

All rights reserved. No part of this publication may be reproduced or utilized in any form or by any
means, electronic or mechanical, including photocopying, recording or by any information storage
and retrieval system, without prior written permission of the publisher.

The authors have asserted their moral rights.

The publishers will be grateful for any information that will assist them in keeping future editions
up to date. Although all reasonable care has been taken in the preparation of this book, neither the
publishers nor the authors can accept any liability for any consequence arising from the use thereof,
or the information contained therein.

ISBN-13: 978 1 84533 245 7

A CIP catalogue record for this book is available from the British Library.

Set in Absara, Frutiger and Goudy

Colour reproduction by United Graphics in Singapore

Printed and bound by Toppan in China

NOTES
This book contains dishes made with raw or lightly cooked eggs and meat. It is prudent for
vulnerable people such as pregnant and nursing mothers, invalids, the elderly, babies and young
children to avoid uncooked or lightly cooked dishes made with eggs and meat.

Meat and poultry should be cooked thoroughly. To test if poultry is cooked, pierce the flesh through
the thickest part with a skewer or fork – the juices should run clear, never pink or red.

Commissioning Editor: Rebecca Spry
Senior Editor: Leanne Bryan
Executive Art Editor: Nicky Collings
Designer: Lizzie Ballantyne
Photographer: Jean-Blaise Hall
Production Controller: Lucy Carter

Introduction   6

Andalucía   10
Aragón   22
Asturias   32
Baleares   42
Canarias   52
Cantabria   62
Castilla y León   72
Castilla-La Mancha   84
Cataluña   96
Extremadura   108
Galicia   118
La Rioja   128
Madrid   140
Murcia   150
Navarra   160
País Vasco   170
Valencia   180

Recommended restaurants   190
Index   192

Since the new constitution of 1978, Spain as a country has returned to the regional cultural diversity it enjoyed in the past, and those of us who have never ventured beyond the Costas may not yet have realized just what this diversity is all about. Nowhere is this more apparent than in gastronomy: Spain's food, wine and other drinks such as *sidra* (cider) and *pacharán* have a strong local cultural heritage, and modern restaurant techniques are bringing classic dishes into the 21st century, just as modern winemaking methods are reinventing the classic Spanish wine areas.

This book is a celebration of the diversity of Spanish culture as seen through its food and drink and its mealtime traditions, always based on the family model and revolving around the *comida*, the most important meal of the day, traditionally eaten at about 2pm after copious tapas and before the siesta. *Comida* simply means 'meal', which shows the importance

Introduction

attached to it. The tradition dates back to the time when schools and businesses started work very early in the morning in the summer and the working day was over by early afternoon, so the family could come together for a meal, before sleeping through the afternoon heat.

The full 'menu' for the Spanish gastronomic day starts with *desayuno* (breakfast), traditionally accompanied by a *café con leche* (milky coffee) and a brandy, which may be mixed together to become a *carajillo* – this is known colloquially as *hacer las camas*: 'to make the beds'. A mid-morning snack is *almuerzo*, which is generally translated as 'lunch' although 'elevenses' might be more accurate.

For those hardy enough to survive the rigours of the *comida* at 2pm, there's always the *merienda*, which roughly equates to afternoon tea, and might be served around 6pm – another light meal to keep you going until dinner-time. In Spain they eat late – seldom before 9pm and often after 10pm, and this is *cena*, which translates as 'dinner' but is probably better described as 'supper'. Although it's a full meal it's usually much lighter than the *comida*. In the days when most Spaniards toiled in the fields all day and every day, some healthy appetites were generated.

In the 21st century this has translated into a wonderful panoply of regional foods, most of them based on the raw materials that were available locally in the days before refrigerated trucks could whisk Galician shellfish to Madrid restaurants overnight. Many of the most popular and intriguing recipes stem from the days when poor families had to be inventive with what few ingredients they could afford. *Migas* from Aragon and Navarra is a good example –

a dish of dry breadcrumbs with whatever was left over from the last meal, perhaps a bit of *chorizo*, ham, cheese, even fruit in some cases, and it's absolutely delicious. Another Spanish staple, *menestra*, is a vegetable stew made with whatever happens to be in season, and is also a relic of these times. The name derives from the Spanish word *menester*, which means 'want' or 'need', illustrating its origins perfectly. Today it's more popular than ever, and rightly so.

There is a saying that 'God created Spain to show the rest of Europe that there is an alternative'. It's certainly true in the kitchen.

ABOUT THE AUTHORS

Mario Sandoval is a phenomenon amongst chefs in Spain. In 2004 he won the national Cooks' Championship and his first Michelin star at the age of 27 – the youngest chef in Spain ever to do so. He is the son and grandson of chefs at the family restaurant Coque at Humanes de Madrid, 28km (18 miles) south-west of Madrid, just off the A42 Madrid–Toledo *Autopista*. He studied in Madrid and Barcelona before taking to the range, and has revolutionized the style and appeal of the restaurant. He represented Spain at the Bocuse d'Or festival in Lyon, and has won many other accolades in his native Madrid, in Spain nationally and beyond. His food style is very much 'modern Spanish' – creating new tastes, styles and recipes that take the best of Spanish regional cookery and reinvent them for the 21st century.

John Radford joined the wine trade in 1972, started lecturing on wine in 1975 and writing about it in 1977. He continued wine-trade consultancy until 1986, after which he went into journalism full time, including radio and television training and, from 1993, BBC radio, first with BBC East and latterly with BBC South-East in Sussex. He now presents a weekly programme on local commercial radio in West Sussex. He writes or has written for most of the food and wine magazines including *Wine International, Decanter, Harpers Wine and Spirit Weekly, BBC Good Food* and many others. His book, *The New Spain* (Mitchell Beazley), won four international awards in 1999. In addition he co-wrote the *Mitchell Beazley Guide to Sweet and Fortified Wines* in 2000 and published *The Wines of Rioja* in 2004 ('Best European Wine Book' at the Livre Gourmand Awards in Versailles, 2005), as well as contributing chapters on Spain and Spanish wine to several guide-books and encyclopedias including the award-winning annual *Wine Report*. In 2005 he was awarded the *Premio Especial de Comunicación, Mejor Labor Informativa Continuada Relacionada Alimentos de España* by the Ministry of Agriculture in Madrid, reflecting his on-going work on Spanish wines.

Abbreviations used in the text:

WINES

DO – *Denominación de Origen*: the main appellation for quality wines in Spain. It guarantees the origin and that certain quality-control checks have been applied

DOCa – *Denominación de Origen Calificada*: a 'higher' appellation for wines of higher quality (there are two – Rioja and Priorat)

DOQ – *Denominació d'Origen Qualificada* (as above but in the Catalan language)

DO de Pago – individual estates (*pagos*) with international acclaim

VCPRD – *Vinos de Calidad Producido en Regiones Determinadas*: a 'junior' version of the DO for wine areas on the way up

VdlT – *Vinos de la Tierra*: country wines

FOOD

The *Denominación de Origen* (DO, as above) is awarded to local produce and ingredients – e.g. ham, cheeses, fruit, olive oil and charcuterie – that have shown consistent excellence over a long period of time. Other regional foods may be styled *Denominación Específica* (DE) or *Indicación Geográfica Protegida* (IGP), which protect the name from use by other regions of Spain.

NAMES AND SPELLINGS

Bodega – a wine producer or wine merchant, or the wine-cellar in a restaurant. Usually in the plural when used as a company name e.g. Bodegas Berberana

Adega – as above but in Galego (Galicia)

Celler – as above but in Catalan (Catalonia)

Cava – as above (Catalonia)

Crianza – wine that has been aged for at least two years, with six months or more in oak

Reserva – wine that has been aged for at least three years, with 12 months or more in oak

Gran Reserva – wine that has been aged for at least five years, with 18 months or more in oak

Unusual equipment and methods:

sifón iSi – a culinary-standard cream-whipping syphon fitted with a nitrous oxide gas cylinder

Roner digital thermostat – a thermostat with a precision temperature control. Useful for sous-vide cooking

sous-vide – the practice of slow-cooking food at precise, low temperatures in vacuum-packed plastic sealable bags. The term is French for 'vacuum-packed'

Thermomix – a food processor that also weighs, cooks, chops, crushes, emulsifies, whips, mixes, steams, blends, kneads, grinds, simmers, grates and mills

A ndalucía (Andalusia), Spain's second-largest region, played a seminal part in the origins of wine in western Europe. The city of Cádiz was founded in 1100BC by Phoenician traders, and colonized around 500BC by Greeks from the eastern Mediterranean, who brought their families, livestock and, most importantly, vines with them. Three hundred years later, the Romans arrived and organized vine-growing and winemaking around modern-day Jerez.

Andalucía's eight provinces include Almería; Granada, the Moorish capital for seven centuries and home of the magnificent Alhambra palace; Málaga; Córdoba, with its magnificent mosque; Jaén; Huelva; and Cádiz, famous for the 1587 raid in which Sir Francis Drake's fleet destroyed the Spanish navy in the harbour. The westernmost province is Sevilla (Seville), the regional capital.

Andalucía specialities are numerous. The region is the virgin olive oil capital of Spain, with 15 established or transitional *denominaciones de origen* (DOs; *see* page 9). There's also a region-wide DO for mackerel and frigate mackerel, which are caught from Almería to Huelva.

Andalucía

Classic cured hams come from Córdoba, Granada and Sierra de Huelva. The last includes the world-famous *jamón de bellota*, from free-range, acorn-fed pigs. *Queso serranía de Ronda* is a goat's cheese made in the highlands of the province of Málaga.

Andalucía doesn't stint on vegetables, either. *Espárrago de Huétor-Tájar* is the asparagus grown in the cool mountains of Granada, and the *tomate de la Cañada-Níjar* of Granada (although technically a fruit) is also included in the list of regional specialities.

In recent years, the wine vinegar produced in Cádiz, Córdoba and Huelva has come to prominence, as TV chefs have discovered the delights of Sherry vinegar in particular.

The most recent fruit DO awarded in the region is *Pasas de Málaga*, which governs the production of giant, juicy Muscatel raisins. *Chirimoya de la Costa Tropical Granada-Málaga* is the DO for custard-apples grown in Granada and Málaga, and the *Cítricos de Huelva* DO covers all manner of citrus fruit, including oranges, grapefruit, mandarins, clemetines and lemons.

In terms of sweets, *miel de Granada*, honey of Granada, has its own DO, while *alfajor de Medina Sidonia* (Sevilla) is a nougat made with honey, almonds, cinnamon and other spices. Finally, Sevilla also offers *mantecada de Estepa*, a traditional Christmas pastry.

This popular dish is Córdoba's take on *gazpacho,* the world-famous chilled tomato soup from southern Spain. Classically, *salmorejo* is made in a mortar or *dornillo* (wooden bowl). Traditionalists insist that the texture is more authentic when it's made by hand, but using a food processor is much quicker. Although this refreshing soup is usually served chilled, it's also delicious when eaten hot in cold weather.

Salmorejo Cordobés

Chilled tomato soup with chopped egg and ham

INGREDIENTS (SERVES 4)

800g (1lb 12oz) very ripe tomatoes

2 garlic cloves, peeled

200g (7oz) day-old bread,
  crusts removed, cut into cubes

125ml (4fl oz) olive oil

1 tablespoon Sherry wine vinegar

salt and freshly ground black
  pepper to taste

GARNISH

2 eggs

1 teaspoon wine vinegar

1 tablespoon olive oil

50g (1¾oz) Iberian ham or
  serrano ham, thinly sliced
  and finely shredded

4 slices of thin, crisp toast
  (optional)

To make the soup, remove any stalks and wash the tomatoes. Chop roughly in a food processor. Then add the garlic and blend again to form a thin tomato purée. Strain through a sieve into a large bowl, and discard the seeds and skin.

Stir the bread into the tomato purée. Set aside to soak for four to 12 hours in the refrigerator. Then pour the tomato and bread mixture into a food processor and blend to a velvety smooth soup with a creamy consistency. Keep the food processor running while slowly drizzling in the olive oil, then the vinegar, a pinch of salt and some black pepper. If necessary, thin the consistency with a few tablespoons of cold water. Pour the *salmorejo* into a bowl and put in the refrigerator to chill.

For the garnish, put the eggs in a saucepan, cover with cold water and add a pinch of salt and a teaspoonful of vinegar. Bring to the boil and cook for 10 minutes. Carefully transfer the eggs to a bowl of iced water to cool quickly. When cold enough to handle, peel off the shells under running water. Part the whites from the yolks before finely chopping both separately.

Ladle a portion of the *salmorejo* into each bowl. Drizzle a few drops of olive oil over the soup. Garnish with a little chopped egg yolk and egg white, strips of ham and a slice of thin, crisp toast, if desired.

WINE TIPS

SPECIAL OCCASION: **Lustau Single Cask Amontillado, Jerez (€€€)**
SUNDAY LUNCH: **Fernando de Castilla Amontillado, Jerez (€€)**
EVERYDAY: **Viña AB, González Byass, Jerez (€)**

The notorious heat of Andalucía influences many of its traditional dishes. Without doubt, the best known are the tasty chilled soups that make good use of locally-grown ingredients, such as almonds and tomatoes. This delicious almond soup reflects the Arab heritage of the region. The provinces of Sevilla and Málaga both claim to have invented it, although similar versions are served all over southern Spain.

Ajo blanco Malagueño

Chilled white almond soup, Málaga-style

INGREDIENTS (SERVES 4)

2 garlic cloves, peeled
150g (5¹/₂oz) blanched almonds, roughly chopped
salt to taste
1 tablespoon Sherry wine vinegar
50ml (2fl oz) olive oil
75g (2³/₄oz) day-old white bread, crusts removed, cut into cubes
500ml (18fl oz) water

GARNISH

olive oil
100g (3¹/₂oz) white grapes
slices of melon

Crush the garlic, almonds and a little salt together in a pestle and mortar to form a smooth paste. Then slowly stir in the vinegar, followed by the olive oil, mixing well. Set aside to chill in the refrigerator overnight to thicken.

Next day, put the bread in a bowl and cover with the water. Leave to soak for 5 minutes, or until softened. Transfer the soggy bread to a food processor. Pour in the almond paste and blend together at high speed, adding any water remaining in the bowl to make a smooth, creamy soup.

Serve the soup in bowls, garnished with a drizzle of olive oil, a few grapes and slices of melon. You could use other combinations of fruit or nuts as a garnish, depending on what you have in the refrigerator.

WINE TIPS

SPECIAL OCCASION: **Amontillado del Duque, González Byass, Jerez (€€€)**
SUNDAY LUNCH: **Pastrana Manzanilla Pasada, Hidalgo, Jerez (€€)**
EVERYDAY: **Tío Pepe, González Byass, Jerez (€)**

In Andalucía, no part of a pig is wasted. Some of the less familiar and cheaper cuts of pork are used to create dishes with outstanding and memorable flavours. The stars of this recipe are the *secreto,* from the side bacon and the *sorpresa*, from the fore shoulder. Their succulent meat marries perfectly with the sweet wine sauce.

Manjar de Ibéricos en diferentes texturas
Iberian charcuterie casserole with a sweet wine sauce

INGREDIENTS (SERVES 4)
450g (1lb) *secreto*
750g (1lb 10oz) *sorpresa*
50g (1¾oz) cooking salt
2 onions, finely chopped
6 carrots, finely chopped
4 leeks, finely chopped
salt and pepper to taste
4 peaches, skinned and sliced
300ml (10fl oz) Montilla or Sherry
   Pedro Ximénez
150ml (5fl oz) water

GARNISH
200g (7oz) morels (mushrooms),
   blanched in boiling water
fresh rosemary or thyme
   (optional)

Wash and trim the *secreto* and *sorpresa*, and keep the trimmings. Rub the salt all over the *secreto* and leave for 1¹/₂ hours. Then wash away the salt under cold running water and dry well. Cut the *secreto* into 1cm- (¹/₂in-) thick slices. Layer the slices into a 900g (2lb) loaf tin, lined with cling film, vacuum-pack into a cooking bag and cook in a *sous-vide* water bath cooker at 70°C (160°F) for at least 10 hours, or until cooked through. Then chill rapidly in the freezer and set aside.

Meanwhile, put the *sorpresa*, 1 of the onions, carrots, leeks and a pinch of salt into a pressure cooker and cover with cold water. Secure the lid, bring to the boil and cook over a low heat for 25 minutes, or until the *sorpresa* is cooked through. Then remove the *sorpresa* and set aside.

Preheat the oven to 150°C (300°F, gas mark 2). Put the pork trimmings and remaining chopped onion in a roasting tin and roast in the oven for 25 minutes until browned and cooked through. After about 20 minutes, add the peaches to the roasting tin. While still hot, transfer the contents of the roasting tin to a saucepan and pour over the wine and water. Bring to the boil and simmer until the liquid has reduced by half. Strain into a clean saucepan and continue boiling until the liquid has thickened to form a sauce.

To prepare the pork for serving, cut the *secreto* into cubes and brown under a low grill and slice the *sorpresa*.

Put some *secreto* on each plate and glaze with a little wine sauce. Arrange a few slices of hot *sorpresa* on the side. Sprinkle a few grains of salt over the meat and garnish with a few morels, glazed with a spoonful of the wine sauce, and fresh rosemary or thyme, if desired.

WINE TIPS
SPECIAL OCCASION: **Ramos Paul, El Chantre, Sierras de Málaga (€€€)**
SUNDAY LUNCH: **Señorío de Nevada Syrah Merlot, Granada Sur-Ouest (€€)**
EVERYDAY: **Reserva Privada, Príncipe Alfonso, Sierras de Málaga (€)**

Those that associate the world of tapas with a wonderfully appetizing array of little dishes of food, which is typical of northern Spain, may be a bit taken aback when they walk into an Andaluz tapas bar for the first time and are confronted with an empty counter. This is because Andaluz tapas are always fried and need to be cooked to order just before serving.

Esturión adobado en gran fritura con mayonesa ligera de lima

Deep-fried sturgeon with lime mayonnaise

INGREDIENTS (SERVES 4)

2 garlic cloves, peeled

salt to taste

1 teaspoon dried oregano

1 teaspoon cumin seeds

3 tablespoons Sherry wine vinegar

pinch of paprika

pinch of ground caraway seeds

2 teaspoons lemon juice

1kg (2lb 4oz) fillet of sturgeon

FOR THE LIME MAYONNAISE

1 egg

salt to taste

2 teaspoons lime juice

200ml (7fl oz) sunflower oil

2 tablespoons olive oil

FOR FRYING

100g (3½oz) chickpea flour

virgin olive oil

GARNISH

finely grated lime rind

fresh herbs (optional)

For a marinade, grind the garlic, a pinch of salt, oregano and cumin seeds in a pestle and mortar to form a paste. Then stir in the vinegar, paprika, ground caraway seeds and lemon juice. Cut the sturgeon fillet into 5cm (2in) strips and coat in the marinade. Keep in the refrigerator for 24 hours.

For the mayonnaise, crack the egg into a bowl. Beat in a pinch of salt and the lime juice. Gradually whisk in the oils, beating vigorously to form a smooth, glossy mayonnaise. Cover with greaseproof paper and set aside in the refrigerator.

Drain the marinade from the sturgeon and coat the pieces of fish in chickpea flour. Heat plenty of virgin olive oil to 180°C (350°F, gas mark 4) in a large saucepan and fry the fish, in batches, for about 8 minutes until crisp on the outside and juicy on the inside. Remove from the saucepan and put on a baking tray lined with kitchen paper to drain off any excess oil.

Arrange 3 or 4 strips of sturgeon in the centre of each plate with a few drops of lime mayonnaise. Garnish with shreds of finely grated lime rind and some fresh herbs, if desired.

WINE TIPS

SPECIAL OCCASION: Sacristia Oloroso Seco, Sánchez Romate, Jerez (€€€)

SUNDAY LUNCH: Blanco de Blancas Nobles, Barranco Oscuro, Contraviesa-Alpujarra (€€)

EVERYDAY: Castillo de San Diego, Barbadillo, Cádiz (€)

Wines of Andalucía

The most famous Andaluz wine is Sherry. Wine has been made in the region around Jerez certainly since about 500BC, and from the Middle Ages to the Victorian era Sherry was widely considered to be the finest wine in the world, largely because, as a fortified wine, it could survive rough handling and primitive transport systems. Until 1933, wine made all over the region was shipped to Jerez and exported under the Sherry name, but in the 20th century, the various wines made outside the Jerez area were renamed according to their individual origins.

DO JEREZ/XÉRÈS/SHERRY Y MANZANILLA DE SANLÚCAR

That's the official full name of this, the Sherry DO, and wine using this *denominación* may be made from grapes (largely Palomino with some Pedro Ximénez (PX) and Moscatel) grown in and around the three towns of Jerez, El Puerto de Santa María and Sanlúcar de Barrameda, in the province of Cádiz. It comes in a number of styles:

Fino is pale, bone-dry and matures under a coating of natural yeast known as *flor*, which gives it a fresh, nutty flavour. It makes an excellent apéritif and is a classic partner for tapas and seafood. It also matches well with spicy oriental dishes. *Finos* made in the coolest area, around Sanlúcar, may be called **manzanilla**.

Amontillado is a *fino* that has been aged for a longer period, and has started to mellow and turn darker in the glass. Still completely dry in their natural state, these wines go well with meat and game. Most commercial *amontillado*, however, is blended with sweetening wines.

Oloroso is a wine that didn't grow a covering of yeast during its maturation period and tends to be a rich walnut-brown in colour. Again, it's completely dry in its natural state, but is very often sweetened and sold as **Cream**.

PX and **Moscatel** are sweet wines made with the named grape: old PX may be almost completely black in colour and is arguably the sweetest wine in the world.

Very old wines may be labelled with an average age: 12, 15, 20 (also VOS – Very Old Sherry) or 30 years (VORS – Very Old Rare Sherry).

DO MONTILLA-MORILES

This is an area in the province of Córdoba which makes traditional fortified wines in the style of Jerez, and with the same names: *fino, amontillado*, etc., but mainly with PX grapes. The style tends to be more robust than Sherry and there are two additional categories: **crianza** wines are unfortified but aged in cask or tank, and **jóvenes** (young wines) are young wines that are bottled straight after the vintage to retain their freshness.

DO MÁLAGA Y SIERRAS DE MÁLAGA

Traditionally, this area made big, sweet, fortified wines whose grapes had been sun-dried before pressing, but the compass is greater now. Unfortified red and white wines are made, typically in the highland areas where the nights are cooler. Sweet wines are labelled *Málaga*, and other wines *Sierras de Málaga*.

DO CONDADO DE HUELVA

In the 19th century this region made Sherry-type wines and sent them to Jerez, but today that is, of course, illegal. They still make fortified styles, almost universally from the Zalema grape. *Pálido* is pale and dry and *viejo* is an aged wine, usually sweetened. In addition there is also a light *joven* wine.

OTHER WINES

Andalucía has 16 Vino de la Tierra (VdlT) areas. Only the most prominent are listed below.

VdlT Cádiz This covers the entire province and allows mainly the Sherry companies to make light, unfortified white wines from the Palomino grape. In recent years, a wider range of grape varieties has been planted and some good wines are being made.

VdlT Contraviesa-Alpujarra This covers an area from the mountains to the coast in the province of Granada, growing a range of grapes. The highland vineyards (over 1,000m/3,300ft) make some excellent whites from Vigiriega and reds from Garnacha, as well as sparkling wines made from both red and white grapes.

VdlT Granada Sur-Ouest As its name implies, this is south-west of the city of Granada, and there are several small bodegas working hard to establish the area with wines made from Syrah, Merlot and Cabernet Sauvignon grapes.

OTHER DRINKS

One of the great classics of Andalucía is Brandy de Jerez: brandy aged in old Sherry casks, often for many years. The base wine for the brandy is, typically, made from the Airén grape grown and distilled in Castilla-La Mancha, although a very few of the finest brandies are distilled from wine made from Palomino grapes grown in Jerez.

The first Brandy de Jerez to carry the name was Fundador by Pedro Domecq, which came onto the market in 1874 and is still a bestseller today. It used to be a tradition in Spain to take a small glass with a cup of coffee with breakfast, a practice known as *hacer las camas* ('to make the beds' – i.e. before going to work), or to mix the brandy with the coffee to make a *carajillo*. Because of its ageing in old Sherry casks, even the cheaper Brandy de Jerez is usually very palatable, but the very best can hold up against any brandy in the world: elegant, mature, fragrant and a perfect, lingering end to an excellent meal. Look for the words *Solera Gran Reserva* on the label, and names with which to conjure include Le Panto (González Byass), Carlos Primero (Pedro Domecq), Conde de Osborne, Cardenal Mendoza (Sánchez Romate), Gran Duque de Alba (Williams & Humbert), and Rey Fernando de Castilla. These are truly sublime.

Main Bodegas

(listed in alphabetical order), PRODUCER NAME; town/village; web/E-mail address; best wines (f = fortified, u = unfortified) A star (*) indicates particularly good quality.

DO JEREZ/XÉRÈS/SHERRY Y MANZANILLA DE SANLÚCAR
www.sherry.org

EMILIO LUSTAU; Jerez; www.emiliolustau.com; Solera range (f), Almacenista range (f)*

GONZÁLEZ BYASS; Jerez; www.gonzalezbyass.es; Tío Pepe (f), VOS/VORS range (f)*, Moncloa range (u)

HIDALGO-LA GITANA; Sanlúcar; www.lagitana.es; La Gitana (f), Pastrana (f)ᴬ, Napoleon range (f)

OSBORNE; El Puerto; www.osborne.es; Fino Quinta (f)*, VOS/VORS range (f)

PEDRO DOMECQ; Jerez; www.domecq.es; Fino la Ina (f)*; Amontillado 51–1ª (f)*, VORS range (f)*

RAINERA PÉREZ MARÍN; Sanlúcar; www.laguita.com; La Guita Manzanilla (f)*, Miraflores range (u)

REY FERNANDO DE CASTILLA; Jerez; www.fernandodecastilla.com; entire range (f)*

SANDEMAN; Jerez; www.sandeman.com; Royal range (f)*

TRADICIÓN; Jerez; www.bodegastradicion.com; entire range (f)*

VALDESPINO; Jerez; www.grupoestevez.com; Inocente (f); Tio Mateo (f)

WILLIAMS & HUMBERT; Jerez; www.williams-humbert.com; Don Zoilo (f), Solera Especial range (f)*

DO MONTILLA-MORILES
www.montilla-moriles.org

ALVEAR; Montilla; www.alvear.es; Capataz (f), CB (f)*, Marques de Montilla (u)

PEREZ BARQUERO; Montilla; www.perezbarquero.com; Gran Barquero (f)

TORO ALBALÁ; Aguilar de la Frontera; www.talbala.com; Eléctrico range (f, u), Don PX (f)*

DO MÁLAGA Y SIERRAS DE MÁLAGA
www.vinomalaga.com

BENTOMIZ; Cómpeta; www.bodegasbentomiz.com; Ariyanas dulce (u)*

DESCALZOS VIEJOS; Ronda; paco@retamero-salesi.com; Descalzos Viejos (u)*

FRIEDRICH SCHATZ; Ronda; www.f-schatz.com; Finca Sanguijela (u)

LÓPEZ HERMANOS; Málaga; www.lopezhermanos.com; entire range (f)*

LOS BUJEOS; Ronda; www.eljuncal.com; Pasos Largos (u)

PRÍNCIPE ALFONSO DE HOHENLOE; Ronda; www.haciendas-espana.com; Príncipe Alfonso (u)

TELMO RODRÍGUEZ; Málaga; cia@fer.es; Molino Real (u)*

DO CONDADO DE HUELVA
www.vinoscondadohuelva.com

OLIVEROS; Bollullos par del Condado; www.bodegasoliveros.com; Viña Oliveros (u), Vino de Pasas (f)

PRIVILEGIO DEL CONDADO; Bollullos par del Condado; www.vinicoladelcondado.com; Prvilegio (u), Misterio (f)

VdlT DE CÁDIZ
See DO Jerez (above)

VdlT CONTRAVIESA-ALPUJARRA

BARRANCO OSCURO; Cádiar; www.barrancooscuro.com; Blancas Nobles (u)*, 1368 Barranco Oscuro (u)*

VdlT GRANADA SUR-OUEST

SEÑORÍO DE NEVADA; Villamena; bodegass_nevada@teleline.es; Señorío de Nevada (u)

Aragón was one of the two independent kingdoms that laid the foundations of modern Spain. In 1469, the future King Ferdinand of Aragón married Queen Isabella of Castilla, which started the process of creating a united Spain. Today, Aragón is a region as famous for its winter sports in the Pyrenees as for its fresh produce and its wines, many of which represent astonishingly good value for money. The capital is the city of Zaragoza, which was founded by the Romans. The region consists of three provinces: Zaragoza, surrounding the capital; Teruel to the south; and Huesca to the north, which shares its northern border with France at the summit of the Pyrenees, including the highest point, Aneto Peak, at 3,404m (11,168ft).

Aragón

LOCAL SPECIALITIES

Jamón de Teruel is the cured ham of the region, made from a local breed of pig that is a Large White/Landrace/Duroc cross. *Ternasco de Aragón* is a local lamb highly admired for its meat and farmed all over the region. Meat products such as *longaniza* (spiced pork sausage), *lomo* (cured pork loin), *morcilla* (black pudding) and *chorizo* (spicy sausage) are produced throughout Aragón. More unusual products include *conserva de cerdo en aceite* (pork loin and rib preserved in olive oil), *cecina* (air-dried or smoked beef) and *ternasco ahumado* (smoked lamb). The *melocotón de Calanda* is a particularly sweet strain of peach grown in the north-east of the province of Teruel. Olives from Caspe in the province of Zaragoza are recognized as a crop in their own right, separate from the oil industry, although *aceite de bajo Aragón* (extra-virgin olive oil) is made in Zaragoza and Teruel; in addition, there's a generic quality mark for the whole region. This is also asparagus country, and the *espárragos de Navarra*, as its name implies, is shared with neighbouring Navarra. The *cebolla dulce de Fuentes* (sweet onion) and the *borraja* (a relative of borage), grow only in the autumn here and in Navarra.

Aragón is one of Spain's leading cheese producers, with both *fresco* (fresh) and *curado* (cured, usually with olive oil) styles as well as *semicurado*. The milk of cows, sheep and goats is used, with *artesanal* styles being the most favoured. *Azafrán de Aragón* (saffron) is one of the most highly prized ingredients in all of Spain – and the most expensive, at approximately €1 (67p) per gram.

Shank of *ternasco* (young lamb) has been a favourite ingredient in this region for many centuries. The tenderness and flavour of the meat is exclusive to sheep reared in the locality. In this recipe, the contrast between the earthy taste of the mushrooms and the sweetness of the figs complements the meat beautifully. Just bear in mind that you may need to order the caul fat from your butcher in advance.

Jarrete de ternasco de Aragón con higos y setas
Tender Aragón lamb shank with figs and mushrooms

INGREDIENTS (SERVES 4)

4 lamb shanks
salt and pepper to taste
1 tablespoon olive oil
2 red peppers, finely chopped
2 green peppers, finely chopped
3 onions, finely chopped
2 garlic cloves, finely chopped
175ml (6fl oz) white wine
175ml (6fl oz) red wine
500ml (18fl oz) beef stock
150g (5¹/₂oz) dried figs (stalks removed), chopped into small pieces
175ml (6fl oz) port
200g (7oz) button mushrooms, washed and sliced
2 tablespoons olive oil
sheet of caul fat, cut into 4 pieces
sprigs of marjoram, to garnish

Season the shanks with salt and pepper. Heat the olive oil in a flameproof casserole and brown the shanks all over. Remove the shanks from the casserole.

In the same oil, gently fry the peppers, onions and garlic for about 15 minutes until softened. Return the shanks to the casserole and pour in the wine and stock. Bring to the boil and simmer until the lamb is tender when pricked with a skewer. Remove the shanks from the casserole and set aside. Strain the juices through a sieve. Set aside to use as the sauce for the dish.

Simmer the figs in the port for about 20 minutes. When the figs are soft and the port reduced, blend into a pulp.

Preheat the oven to 170°C (325°F, gas mark 3). Spread the mushrooms on a baking tray, drizzle over 1 tablespoon of olive oil and a sprinkling of salt. Roast in the oven for 25 minutes. Drain off any juices. Heat 1 tablespoon of olive oil in a frying pan and sauté the mushrooms briefly until just browned.

Gently twist the bones out of the shanks, disturbing the meat as little as possible. Spread out the caul fat and use 1 sheet to wrap up each piece of meat, wrapping the fat several times around the meat to make it thicker, forming 4 neat cylinders. Stand the cylinders on a baking tray and roast in the oven at 170°C (325°F, gas mark 3) for 3 minutes.

Place a spoonful of the fig pulp and sautéed mushrooms on each plate, and sit the shank beside. Glaze the top of the shank with a little sauce and drizzle a little more around the plate. Garnish with a sprig of fresh marjoram.

WINE TIPS

SPECIAL OCCASION: **Blecua, Viñas del Vero, Somontano (€€€)**
SUNDAY LUNCH: **Fagús Coto de Hayas, Aragonesas, Campo de Borja (€€)**
EVERYDAY: **Imperial Carinus Reserva, San Valero, Cariñena (€)**

Aragón is a fertile region, blessed with many rivers, and famous for growing magnificent vegetables. The markets are stacked with onions from Fuentes de Ebro, beetroot from Jalón, garlic from Bardallur and cardoons (artichoke thistles) from Muel and Mozota. The mildness of *borrajas*, a green leafy vegetable first introduced to Spain from Africa by the Arabs, suits the mix of earthy and salty flavours in this soup perfectly.

Tallos de borrajas con arroz y almejas
Borrajas stems with rice and clams

INGREDIENTS (SERVES 4)

300g (10¹/₂oz) *borrajas* stems (a green leaf with long white stems, similar to Swiss chard)

2 tablespoons olive oil

4 garlic cloves, peeled and chopped

1 tablespoon flour

1 litre (1³/4 pint) fish stock

1 tablespoon chopped fresh parsley

30g (1oz) rice

250g (9oz) fresh clams (shells on)

salt and freshly ground black pepper to taste

Wash the *borrajas* and shred the leaves. Heat the olive oil in a large saucepan and fry the garlic until golden. Then sprinkle in the flour and mix into the olive oil with a wooden spoon. Cook for 2 minutes over a moderate heat.

Add the fish stock, stirring continuously with a whisk, so that lumps do not form, then add the chopped parsley. When the stock starts to boil, add the *borrajas* and rice. Boil over a high heat for 15 minutes.

Then tip in the clams, cover the saucepan and continue boiling for 3–4 minutes until the shells open. Turn off the heat, add a pinch of salt and a few twists of pepper and stir well.

Ladle some of the *borrajas* and rice soup into each bowl. Scatter the clams on top.

WINE TIPS

SPECIAL OCCASION: **Reyes de Aragón Ecológico Blanco, Calatayud (€€€)**
SUNDAY LUNCH: **Viñas del Vero Clarión Blanco, Somontano (€€)**
EVERYDAY: **Care Blanco Chardonnay, Bodegas Añadas, Cariñena (€)**

Poultry is a great speciality of Aragón, and this chicken stew is among the region's best-loved dishes. From village to village, it appears in many guises, but it's always the superb flavour of the rich red pepper, tomato and onion sauce that lingers in the memory. Such tasty juices are just perfect for mopping up with lots of crusty bread.

Pollo al Chilindrón

Chicken stew, Chilindrón-style

INGREDIENTS (SERVES 4)

3 tablespoons olive oil

4 red peppers, washed and dried

1 large chicken, washed and
    jointed into 2 breasts and
    2 legs

salt and freshly ground black
    pepper to taste

3 garlic cloves, chopped

2 onions, finely chopped

150g (5 1/2oz) piece of Iberian ham,
    or *serrano* ham, diced

400g (14oz) tin chopped tomatoes

spring onions, finely sliced,
    to garnish

Preheat the oven to 180°C (350°F, gas mark 4). Rub 1 tablespoon of olive oil over the peppers. Put on a baking tray and roast in the oven for 15 minutes. Set aside to cool, then peel and cut into 1cm (1/2in) strips.

Season the chicken pieces with salt and pepper. Heat the remaining 2 tablespoons of olive oil in a flameproof casserole over a medium heat. Add the chicken and brown on all sides, then remove from the casserole and set aside.

In the same casserole, lightly fry the garlic, onions and ham. When lightly browned, add the tomatoes and strips of pepper, and return the chicken pieces to the pot. Stir everything together well. Bring to the boil over a medium heat and simmer over a low heat for about 40 minutes, stirring from time to time, until the chicken is tender and cooked through. Adjust the seasoning if necessary.

Spoon a generous quantity of the red pepper and tomato sauce onto the centre of each plate. Lay a chicken piece on top, slightly to one side. Garnish with a sprinkling of spring onions.

WINE TIPS

SPECIAL OCCASION: **Marboré, Pirineos, Somontano (€€€)**
SUNDAY LUNCH: **Tres Picos, Borsao, Campo de Borja (€€)**
EVERYDAY: **Baltasar Gracián Garnacha Viñas Viejas, San Alejandro, Calatayud (€)**

The fruit that grows in Aragón is the inspiration for numerous delicious desserts. This recipe showcases the versatility of just one fruit: the apple. By using different varieties of apple and a range of cooking techniques, a refreshing dish of creamy and melting textures with sweet and sour flavours is created to delight the taste buds.

Bomba de manzana con crema ahumada de manzana caramelizada y gelatina de sidra

Apple cream bun with apple sorbet and cider jelly

INGREDIENTS (SERVES 4)

FOR THE CIDER JELLY
500ml (18fl oz) sweet cider
3 sheets of leaf gelatine, soaked

FOR THE APPLE SORBET
700ml (1¼ pint) water
300g (10½oz) brown sugar
6 Granny Smith apples, peeled, quartered and cored

FOR THE APPLE BUN
½kg (1lb 2oz) Bramley apples
50g (1¾oz) sugar
80g (2¾oz) butter
250ml (9fl oz) cider
6 sheets of leaf gelatine, soaked
350ml (12fl oz) double cream

FOR THE LIGHT SYRUP
350ml (12fl oz) water
150g (5½oz) brown sugar

For the cider jelly, heat the cider gently in a saucepan. When hot but not boiling, stir in the gelatine. Continue heating and stirring gently until the sheets have dissolved. Pour into a shallow dish. Leave to cool before putting the jelly in the refrigerator to set overnight. Before serving, cut the jelly into small cubes and keep in the refrigerator.

For the apple sorbet, heat the water and sugar gently in a saucepan. Boil the syrup until it becomes a light brown colour, then allow to cool. Blend the apples with the syrup to a smooth purée in a food processor. Pour into a plastic container and put in the freezer overnight until frozen.

For the apple buns, roast the apples in the sugar and butter at 180°C (350°F, gas mark 4) for 20 minutes. Halfway through the cooking time, pour in the cider. When the apples are cooked, spoon the pulp and remaining cider into a large bowl and discard the skin, core and pips. Add the gelatine and stir until the sheets have dissolved. Leave to cool.

Whip the cream and fold it into the cooled apple mixture. Pour the apple cream into a plastic container, cover and leave to set overnight in the refrigerator.

For the light syrup, heat the water and sugar gently in a saucepan. Boil the syrup until it becomes a light brown colour, then allow to cool.

Drizzle a trail of light syrup across the middle of each plate. Use an ice-cream scoop to shape a ball from the apple cream. Place this apple 'bun' on one side of the syrup line. Put a scoop of apple sorbet on the other side, and arrange a pile of cider jelly cubes in between.

WINE TIPS

SPECIAL OCCASION: **Gewurztraminer, Enate, Somontano (€€€)**
SUNDAY LUNCH: **Coto de Hayas Moscatel, Aragonesas, Campo de Borja (€€)**
EVERYDAY: **Moscatel Ainzón, Santo Cristo, Campo de Borja (€)**

Wines of Aragón

Aragón has four DO wine areas, three in Zaragoza province and the fourth high in the Pyrenees in the province of Huesca. The last makes wines from mainly international varieties such as Cabernet Sauvignon and Merlot, although Tempranillo is widespread throughout the region. The three Zaragozano DOs – Calatayud, Campo de Borja and Cariñena – languished in terms of exports until discovering that their ancient plantations of Garnacha and Cariñena could produce wonderful quality wines if the local cooperatives harvested at lower yields. Eventually, some co-ops merged and became limited companies, which allowed them to offer better prices for grapes from older vineyards. Many growers discovered they could produce half as much and get more money for their production. These are now some of the best-value wines in Spain. Sparkling wines are also made under the Cava DO; *see* Cataluña, page 105.

DO CALATAYUD

DO Calatayud is the southernmost of the Aragonés wine areas, based around the town of the same name. It was the first to exploit low-yielding old vines and to amalgamate old cooperatives into dynamic new companies.

DO CAMPO DE BORJA

DO Campo de Borja is a continuation southwards of the Navarra DO into a more arid area but still well supplied with plantations of old vines.

DO CARIÑENA

DO Cariñena is almost as big as all other Aragonés wine areas put together. Its wines offer consistently good value for money at the budget end of the market.

DO SOMONTANO

DO Somontano is the most recent wine area in Aragón, high in the Pyrenees. The winemaking style here is completely different from the rest of Aragón, centred around international varieties, as well as Tempranillo and Garnacha.

OTHER WINES

VdlT Bajo Aragón Teruel (mainly) and Zaragoza: an improving area with some encouraging new investment. The best wines are red and mainly Garnacha, with some Tempranillo, Cabernet Sauvignon and Syrah.

VdlT Ribera del Queiles Zaragoza: a new venture. Only one notable bodega makes wine both here and across the border to the east in Navarra (*see* Navarra, page 168).

VdlT Valle del Cinca Huesca: another new venture driven by a major wine company – Codorníu from Cava country in the Cinca river valley.

Other wines of mainly local interest, although with the odd rising star, are made in the **VdlTs Valdejalón** (Zaragoza), **Campo de Belchite** (Zaragoza and Teruel), **Muniesa** (Teruel), **Ribera del Gállego-Cinco Villas** (Zaragoza) and **Tierra Baja de Aragón** (Zaragoza).

OTHER DRINKS

The small village of Colungo in Huesca (pop. 179) is a distillation centre for spirits made from leftover grape pomace (www.aguardientescolungo.com). The basic spirit is *orujo* (as in Galicia), available as 'natural' and oak-aged in barrel. It's also made with herbs, coffee, tea, fruit, flowers and anis, in the style of *Patxaran* (*see* Navarra, page 169).

Main Bodegas

(listed in alphabetical order), PRODUCER NAME; town/village; web/E-mail address; best wines (r = red, w = white, p = pink) A star (*) indicates particularly good quality.

DO CALATAYUD
www.docalatayud.com.

JALÓN; Calatayud; www.castillodemaluenda.com; Castillo de Maluenda (r), Claraval (r)*

LANGA; Calatayud; www.bodegas-langa.com; Reyes de Aragón (r)

SAN ALEJANDRO; Miedes; www.san-alejandro.com; Viñas de Miedes (r), Baltasar Gracián (r)*

SAN GREGORIO; Cervera de la Cañada; www.bodegasangregorio.com; Monte Armantes (r)

DO CAMPO DE BORJA
www.campodeborja.com

ALTO MONCAYO; Bulbuente; www.bodegasaltomoncayo.com; Alto Moncayo (r), Aquilón (r)*

ARAGONESAS; Fuendejalón; www.bodegasaragonesas.com; Coto de Hayas (r), Fagús (r)*

BORDEJE; Ainzón; www.bodegasbordeje.com; Don Pablo (r), Pago de Romeroso (r)

BORSAO; Borja; www.bodegasborsao.com; Borsao (r), Tres Picos (r)*

SANTO CRISTO; Ainzón; www.bodegas-santo-cristo.com; Peñazuela (r), Viña Ainzón Reserva (r)

DO CARIÑENA
www.docarinena.com

AÑADAS; Cariñena; www.carewines.com; Care (r, w)*

GRANDES VINOS; Cariñena; www.grandesvinos.com; Monasterio de las Viñas (r), Corona de Aragón (r)

GRAN DUCAY; Cariñena; www.bodegasanvalero.com; Monte Ducay (r), Carinus (r)*

SEÑORÍO DE AYLÉS; Mezalocha; www.bodegasayles.com; Aylés (r)

SOLAR DE URBEZO; Cariñena; www.solardeurbezo.es; Urbezo (r)

VICTORIA; Cariñena; www.bodegasvictoria.com; Dominio de Longaz (r), Longus (r)*

DO SOMONTANO
www.somontano.com

ENATE; Salas Bajas; www.enate.es; Enate (r, w, p), Merlot-Merlot (r)*

IRIUS; Barbastro; www.bodegairius.com; Absum (r, w)

LALANNE; Barbastro; www.bodegaslalanne.com; Lalanne (r), Leonor (r), Laura (r)

OSCA; Ponzano; www.bodegasosca.com; Osca (r), L'Ainsa (r)

OTTO BESTUÉ; Enate; www.bodega-ottobestue.com; Bestué (r, p), Finca Santa Sabina (r)*

PIRINEOS; Barbastro; www.bodegapirineos.com; Montesierra (r, w, p), Pirineos (r, w, p)

VIÑAS DEL VERO; Barbastro; www.vinasdelvero.com; Viñas del Vero (r, w, p), Gran Vos (r)*, Blecua (r)*

VdIT BAJO ARAGÓN

DOMINIO MAESTRAZGO; Alcorisa; www.dominiomaestrazgo.com; Dominio Maestrazgo (r), Rex Deus (r)*

VdIT RIBERA DEL QUEILES

GUELBENZU; Vierlas; www.guelbenzu.com; Guelbenzu Vierlas (r)

VdIT VALLE DEL CINCA

NUVIANA; San Miguel-Belver de Cinca; www.nuviana.com; Nuviana (r)

Asturias is unique in Spain in being a *principado* (principality) rather than an *autonomía* (autonomous region), and its capital is the city of Oviedo. Its heritage is Celtic, and the heir to the Spanish throne has, since 1388, been styled 'Prince of the Asturias', rather as the heir to the British throne has, since 1301, been styled 'Prince of Wales'. When the Moors ruled most of mainland Spain, Asturias became a reservoir of the Christian royalty of Castilla y León, not to mention the springboard for the revolt that eventually became the *Reconquista* – ultimately, the foundation of a united Spain.

Asturias

The region's prosperity was founded in coal and iron mining, but today its green, cool, mountainous area is rich in pastureland, culminating in the spectacular Picos de Europa, including the 2,648m (8,738ft) peak of Torrecerredo. The coastline fronts the Bay of Biscay and, along with neighbouring Galicia and Cantabria, boasts some of the longest and cleanest beaches in Europe. Gastronomically, it's a seafood region, with particular centres of excellence at Oviedo and Gijón.

LOCAL SPECIALITIES

Cattle farming dominates this almost alpine region and *ternera asturiana* is the beef from the local Asturiana de los Valles and Asturiana de las Montañas breeds, or crosses between them. The cattle lead an almost free-range life in the mountain valleys, are fed on local cereals, vegetables, soya and sunflower seeds, among other produce, during their first five months, and are slaughtered at 12 or 18 months old.

Where there are cattle, there's cheese, and Asturias produces five listed cheeses. The most famous is *Cabrales*, made from raw cow's milk (with an admixture of sheep's and goat's milk) and matured in mountain caves to develop its characteristic blue-green veins. Another is *afuega'l pitu*, which, in the local dialect, means 'to choke the chicken'. It's a soft cow's-milk cheese; to test its readiness, farmers would feed it to a chicken. If the chicken swallowed it, it was ready to sell. If the chicken choked, it was still too hard. Other cheeses include *beyos*, a hard cow's-milk cheese sometimes with an admixture of goat's and sheep's milk, and lightly smoked; *gamonedo*, a hard cheese, also lightly smoked and made with milk from all three animals; and *vidiago*, a soft, creamy, cow's-milk cheese made in the east of the region.

The 'national dish' of Asturias is *fabada Asturiana*, a rich stew made with the local large white *faba Asturiana* (*fava*) beans, *chorizo*, *morcilla* (black pudding), shoulder of pork and saffron. Despite the humble ingredients, its complex blend of flavours and textures has achieved almost mythical status. Perhaps better than any other dish, this rustic stew exemplifies the simple perfection of traditional Spanish cooking.

Fabada Asturiana
White-bean stew with assorted pork cuts

INGREDIENTS (SERVES 4)

1kg (2lb 4oz) dried white beans (haricot)
300g (10¹/₂oz) pork shoulder
100g (3¹/₂oz) piece of Iberian ham or *serrano* ham
2 *chorizo* sausages, 15cm (6in) long
2 *morcillas* (black puddings), 15cm (6in) long
¹/₂ onion
1 carrot
a few strands of saffron
sprigs of flatleaf parsley, to garnish (optional)

Soak the beans overnight in plenty of cold water. In another bowl, soak the pork shoulder and ham overnight as well.

Drain the beans and tip into a large saucepan. Cover with fresh cold water. Bring to the boil, then simmer over a low heat for about 1 hour, skimming off any residue that rises to the surface.

After this time, add the rest of the ingredients and cover with more cold water. Bring back to the boil and simmer over a low heat for 2 hours, or until the meats are cooked through. Stir gently from time to time, taking care to keep the beans whole.

Remove the meats, sausages, black puddings and vegetables from the pan, cut them into small pieces, to produce a mixture known as *compango*, and set aside. Ladle some beans and sauce into deep bowls. Then add a selection of the *compango*. Garnish with sprigs of flatleaf parsley, if desired.

WINE TIPS

SPECIAL OCCASION: **Tares P3, Dominio de Tares, Bierzo (€€€)**
SUNDAY LUNCH: **Abadía da Cova Tinto, Moure, Ribeira Sacra (€€)**
EVERYDAY: **Sidra de Asturias (€)**

Asturian food is a model of simplicity, combining fresh locally grown ingredients to produce dishes with remarkably bold flavours. True to form, when the local cider, which is drunk in most *chigres* (bars) in the region, is used to make a sauce for freshly caught hake, the result has a sensationally piquant and original taste. The same sauce works well with any firm white fish.

Merluza a la sidra

Hake with cider sauce

INGREDIENTS (SERVES 4)
8 large clams (shells on)
4 hake fillets
4 prawns

FOR THE SAUCE
1 tablespoon virgin olive oil
1 onion, finely chopped
2 garlic cloves, finely chopped
1 tablespoon plain flour
250ml (9fl oz) dry cider
2 spring onions, finely chopped
salt and freshly ground black
    pepper to taste

GARNISH
sprigs of parsley
slices of apple, rubbed in lemon
    juice to prevent discolouring

To make the sauce, heat the olive oil in a frying pan and fry the onion and garlic gently until soft and golden. Sprinkle in the flour and mix well into the olive oil with a wooden spoon. Pour in the cider, stirring all the time, until the sauce has boiled and is slightly thickened. Just before taking the frying pan off the heat, stir in the spring onions and season with salt and pepper.

Tip the sauce into a food processor and blend until smooth. Strain the sauce through a sieve and pour it back into the frying pan.

Bring back to the boil over a low heat before adding the clams. When the clam shells open, remove from the heat. Discard any clam shells that do not open.

Meanwhile, grill the hake under a medium grill for 10 minutes. Grill the prawns for the last 3 minutes.

Spoon a little sauce into the bottom of each dish, then place the hake, 1 prawn and 2 clams on top. Garnish with sprigs of parsley and slices of apple.

WINE TIPS
SPECIAL OCCASION: **Casal Caeiro Vendimia Seleccionada, Rías Baixas (€€€)**
SUNDAY LUNCH: **Monasterio de Corias, Vinos Cangas, Cangas (€€)**
EVERYDAY: **Sidra de Asturias (€)**

Roasted meats are very popular in Asturia, especially when served with a cheese sauce, made from the local blue cheese, known as *Cabrales*, or a homemade cheese, such as *afuega'l pitu*, a type of creamy feta-style cheese. Others use plenty of cider in their cooking. This recipe skilfully plays around with traditional ideas to produce a fusion of flavours that would leave any food-lover wanting more.

Cabrito en adobo con patatitas maceradas en reducción de sidra

Marinated kid with new potatoes in a cider sauce

INGREDIENTS (SERVES 4)

3 garlic cloves
fresh parsley, chopped
1.5kg (3lb 5oz) kid, on the bone
sprigs of rosemary and thyme
3 tablespoons olive oil, plus extra
    for frying
200ml (7fl oz) white wine
100g (3½oz) red *afuega'l pitu*
    cheese or cream cheese
2 eggs, beaten
55g (2oz) plain flour

FOR THE SAUCE

2 leeks, chopped
1 onion, chopped
2 carrots, chopped
rosemary, bay and thyme
500ml (18fl oz) dry cider

FOR THE POTATOES

500ml (18fl oz) dry cider
4 small potatoes, cut in half, with a
    hole in the middle of each piece
115g (4oz) kid's liver, sliced

Grind the garlic and parsley together in a pestle and mortar to form a paste. Chop the kid into pieces then rub the paste into the kid and leave to marinate for 12 hours in the refrigerator.

Arrange the pieces of kid in an ovenproof dish with the rosemary, thyme, 2 tablespoons of the olive oil and the white wine. Roast in the oven at 130°C (250°F, gas mark ½) for 50 minutes, so that the meat stays moist.

Remove the kid from the oven and leave to cool. When cold, take the meat off the bones and crumble into pieces. Save the bones for making the sauce later. Mix the cheese into the meat and roll into a 'sausage' shape. Wrap in cling film and freeze overnight. Cut the meaty cheese sausage into 4 pieces. Dip each piece in the egg, then the flour, and fry over a high heat in lots of olive oil until brown. Set aside.

For the sauce, heat 1 tablespoon olive oil in a large saucepan. Tip in the kid bones and brown over a high heat. Throw in the vegetables and herbs, and pour in the cider. Simmer over a very low heat, adding water as required, for 5 hours. Then strain the stock into a clean saucepan. Return to the heat and reduce to a thick glossy sauce.

For the potatoes, bring the cider to the boil in a saucepan, then simmer over a medium heat until reduced by half. Drop in the potatoes and boil for 20 minutes until cooked. Fry the slices of kid's liver in a little olive oil in a frying pan for 1–2 minutes on each side, depending on the thickness of the slices, then crush to form a coarse pâté. Carefully stuff the liver pâté into each potato.

Spoon a little cider sauce into each dish. Arrange a kid/cheese roll on one side of the pool and 2 pieces of stuffed potato on the other.

WINE TIPS

SPECIAL OCCASION: **Tilenus Pagos de Posada, Estefanía, Bierzo (€€€)**
SUNDAY LUNCH: **Peregrino, Gordonzello, León (€€)**
EVERYDAY: **Sidra de Asturias (€)**

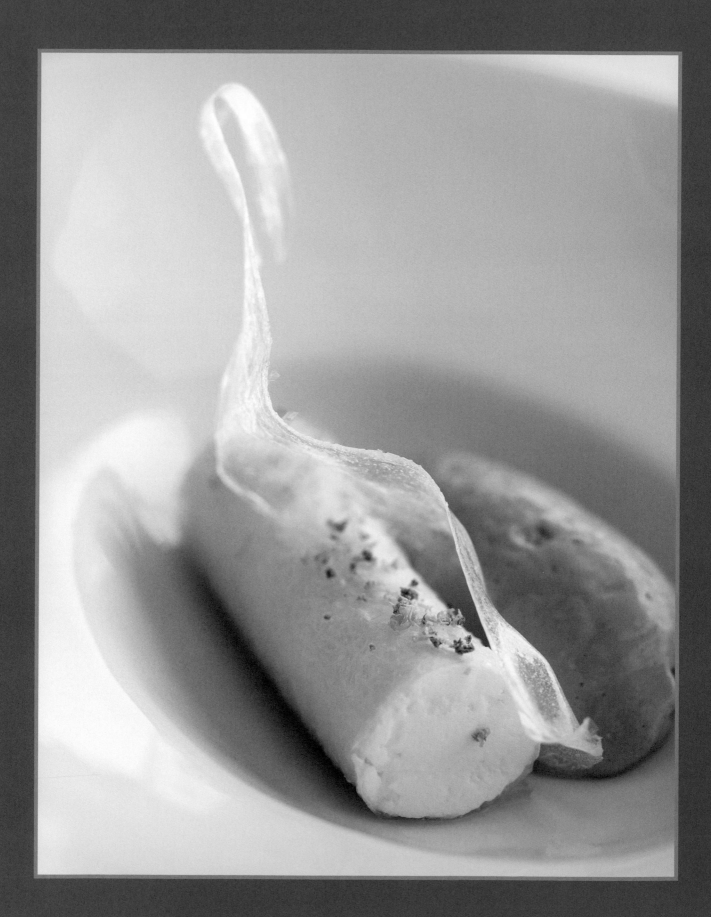

In the 15th century, Sephardic Jews brought rice to Asturias. By a happy coincidence, rice goes very well with the creamy local milk to create the region's signature dessert: rice pudding. Traditionally, it is made with just rice and milk, topped with caramel. Introducing cinnamon, star anise and lemon as well, and the stunning new presentation, adds textures and flavours to tantalize the taste buds.

Arroz con leche Asturiano con helado de canela y crujiente de limón

Rice pudding Asturias-style with cinnamon ice cream and crunchy lemon

INGREDIENTS (SERVES 4)

FOR THE RICE PUDDING
75g (2³/4oz) short-grain rice, rinsed
100ml (3¹/2fl oz) water
1 litre (1³/4 pint) full-fat milk
125ml (4fl oz) double cream
grated rind of half an orange
150g (5¹/2oz) caster sugar
55g (2oz) butter
500ml (18fl oz) whipping cream

FOR THE ANISEED GLAZE
500ml (18fl oz) water
4 star anise
1 teaspoon powdered gelatine

FOR THE ICE CREAM
325ml (11fl oz) full-fat milk
325ml (11fl oz) whipping cream
100g (3¹/2oz) caster sugar
2 cinnamon sticks
2 egg yolks
1 teaspoon ground cinnamon

FOR THE CRUNCHY LEMON
1 lemon, very thinly sliced
caramel syrup

For the rice pudding add the rice to a saucepan with the water and bring to the boil. Once the water has evaporated, add the milk, cream and orange rind. Simmer over a low heat for 1 hour, stirring occasionally. Remove from the heat, stir in the sugar and butter and set aside to cool before putting in the refrigerator.

Whip the cream to a medium stiffness and fold into the cold rice pudding. Pour the rice into a rectangular dish, about 20 x 10cm (8 x 4in) and 1.5cm (⁵/8in) deep. Put in the refrigerator to set. When ready to roll in the aniseed glaze below, turn the block of creamed rice out onto a chopping board and cut into 4 bars.

For the glaze, boil the water with the star anise and add the gelatine. Pour into a tray to create a thin sheet of jelly and allow to cool before putting in the refrigerator. When set, remove from the tray, cut into 4 strips and roll around the bars of rice pudding, creating sweet 'cannelloni'. Trim the ends to neaten and chill until needed.

To make the cinnamon ice cream, put the milk, cream, sugar and cinnamon sticks in a saucepan. Gently heat to 50°C (120°F), stirring to make sure the sugar dissolves. Then whisk in the egg yolks and cinnamon. Continue stirring until the temperature rises to 85°C (185°F). Remove from the heat and set aside to cool, then pour into a plastic container and put in the freezer until needed.

Place a roll of rice and anise glaze 'cannelloni' on one side of each dish, and a scoop of cinnamon ice cream on the other. Decorate the ice cream with the crunchy lemon slices. The image shows an optional lemon and lime garnish.

For the crunchy lemon, soak the lemon slices in caramel syrup then place in the oven at 110°C (225°F, gas mark ¹/4) to dry for 3 hours, or until they are crunchy.

WINE TIPS

SPECIAL OCCASION: **Gallaecia, Martín Códax, Rías Baixas (€€€)**
SUNDAY LUNCH: **Liberalia Uno, Liberalia Enológica, Toro (€€)**
EVERYDAY: **Sweet Sidra de Asturias (€)**

Wines of Asturias

Asturias has only one wine area, created in 2001: the Vino de la Tierra de Cangas (www.vinotierracangas.com), in the south-west of the region around the town of Cangas del Narcea. For many years this was an area of domestic winemaking with the odd cottage-industry bodega, but since 2001 some half-dozen bodegas have been making wine on a (usually small) commercial scale. Interestingly, the grapes grown here are mainly unique to Asturias: Albarín Negro, Albarín Blanco (not, they insist, the Albariño of neighbouring Galicia), Verdejo Tinto and Carrasquín Tinto as well as the slightly more familiar Picapoll Blanco, Albillo, Moscatel of Alexandria and Mencía. Understandably, given the northern climate and seafood culture along the coast of the Bay of Biscay, the whites tend to be better than the reds.

OTHER DRINKS

Asturias is nationally famous for *sidra de Asturias*: i.e. cider (www.sidradeasturias.es). Orchards dominate the north-east of the region, with a concentration along the coast; many cider-apple varieties are unique to Asturias, with names such as Durona de Tresali, Limón Montés, Teórica, Raxao, Xuanina, Fuentes, Verdialona and Ernestina. Traditionally, the apples are crushed in a wooden trough using wooden mallets and shovels; the juice is then run off into barrels where it ferments for five to seven months. The producer then blends the different barrels to get the right mix of sweetness and acidity before bottling without filtration. Both still and sparkling ciders are made, the latter by natural fermentation in the bottle, and the style is very refreshing (usually quite dry); they are traditionally drunk with *fabada Asturiana*.

Because most traditional ciders have a sediment in the bottle, Asturians have developed a method of pouring called *el escanciado*, which involves holding the bottle horizontally to trap the sediment and pouring from a great height to aerate the cider. This is accomplished by holding the bottle up at arm's length over the head and pouring into a glass held in the other hand. A variation on this is a bodily contortion in which the glass is held behind the back and the bottle poured over the shoulder. It's a matter of skill and great pride to do this without spillage. Some cafés and bars have a mechanism on the wall that does this by pulling a string that tilts the bottle, but this is considered unromantic by traditionalists.

Main Bodegas

(listed in alphabetical order), PRODUCER NAME; town/village; web/E-mail address; best wines (r = red, w = white) A star (*) indicates particularly good quality.

VINOS CANGAS; Cangas del Narcea; www.bodegacorias.com; Monasterio de Corias (w)

Baleares (The Balearic Islands) comprise the inhabited islands (in order of size) of Majorca, Minorca, Ibiza, Formentera and Cabrera, the last of which is a nature reserve. There are also several small uninhabited islands that are havens for wildlife. Politically, all the islands are grouped together as the province and *autonomía of Illes Balears*.

The Baleares have been a trading post and military base for centuries, although the invaders since the 1960s have had more peaceable ambitions. Well away from the tourist areas, most islands are stunningly beautiful. Majorca has the Serra de Tramuntana ('Mountains of the North Wind') range along its north coast – including the island's highest peak, Puig Major (1,450m/4,757ft) – rolling plains in the centre (where most of the best vineyards are found) and, of course, small unspoiled fishing ports and dramatic bays with endless beaches. Minorca is the furthest east and has the most beguiling coves and estuaries around its coastline, with a large natural harbour at Mahón, the island's capital and reputedly the birthplace of the now-ubiquitous mayonnaise sauce, known here as *mahonesa*. Ibiza is much

Baleares

smaller but has a cliff-faced coastline with narrow caves on the north coast. Formentera and Cabrera are smaller still, and the nature reserve on Cabrera is only accessible by special permit.

LOCAL SPECIALITIES

The climate is mild and Mediterranean, and the gastronomy very varied. Cheese is a major industry, with *Mahón-Menorca* the most popular, made from raw cow's milk and often rubbed with oil and paprika for extra flavour. Soft when young, it becomes harder with age; Mahón reserva/semicurado is probably the best. Olive oil is a feature of Majorca, made from Mallorquina, Arbequina and Picual varieties. The oil tends to be fruity when young, ageing to a subtle sweetness when mature. Meat products are a major feature, and *sobrassada de Mallorca* is a favourite spicy sausage, rather like *chorizo* but softer, with a characteristic local flavour. It comes in two styles: *sobrassada* and *sobrassada porc negre*; the latter is made from the meat of black pigs. In the pastry department, the *ensaimada de Mallorca* is made with flour, water, sugar, eggs and pork lard (everyone has a secret recipe for the amounts), rolled out into a long, thin cylinder, and then wound around into a flat disc before baking. There's a variant that is made as above, but stuffed with angel-hair pasta.

This hearty Mediterranean stew is well loved in the Balearic Islands, especially on Ibiza. An assortment of meats is used in this version but it's just as tasty and nourishing when made with a selection of fish instead. *Bullit* is still enjoyed in two servings: first a bowl of meat, vegetables and pulses, followed by another of rice. Some *alioli*, a garlic mayonnaise, on the side, livens up the stew no end.

Bullit

Traditional rice stew with assorted meats or fish

INGREDIENTS (SERVES 4)

250g (9oz) dried chickpeas

150g (5½oz) piece of streaky
    bacon

1 ham bone

1 veal shin bone

500g (1lb 2oz) shoulder of lamb,
    off the bone

½ cabbage, cut into 2 pieces

4 potatoes, peeled and quartered

1 onion, quartered

1 tomato, halved

1 celery stick, chopped

200g (7oz) *sobrassada*, (Majorcan
    sausage – similar to *chorizo*)

1 *morcilla* (black pudding),
    15cm (6in) long

500g (1lb 2oz) *calasparra* rice

pinch of saffron

salt to taste

GARNISH

fried dried red pepper

extra-virgin olive oil with garlic

The night before preparing the stew, put the chickpeas in a bowl of cold water to soak and wash the bacon well.

In a large saucepan, place the bones, lamb and bacon. Drain the chickpeas and add to the saucepan, then cover with cold water. Bring to the boil, put a lid on the saucepan and leave to cook over a low heat for 2 hours, or until the meats are cooked through. Skim the surface several times during cooking to remove any residue that rises to the surface.

After 2 hours, add the cabbage, potatoes, onion, tomato and celery. Put the lid back on, return to the boil and cook for 15 minutes more. Then add the *sobrassada*, *morcilla* and rice. Replace the lid, bring back to the boil again and cook over a moderate heat for another 15 minutes. Stir in the saffron and salt, reduce the heat to low and leave for a further 5 minutes.

Remove the *sobrassada*, *morcilla*, bacon, meats and vegetables from the pan. Cut the sausages and meat into bite-size pieces.

Serve the stew in the traditional manner – first, bowls of meat, chickpeas and vegetables garnished with slices of fried dried red pepper, then bowls of rice, seasoned with drizzles of garlic oil.

WINE TIPS

SPECIAL OCCASION: Gran Vinya Son Caules, Miquel Gelabert, Pla i Llevant (€€€)

SUNDAY LUNCH: Buc, Jaume de Puntiró, Binissalem (€€)

EVERYDAY: Macià Batle Añada Tinto, Binissalem (€)

Mahón cheese plays an indispensable part in Minorcan cooking. The square cheeses with their distinctive orange rind have been made by hand on the island for more than 2,000 years. The cheese itself is yellowish, with a firm texture and the slightly sweet taste of fresh milk. As this simple recipe proves, it's best eaten on its own or with some ham, tomatoes and olives – and plenty of fresh crusty bread.

Queso fresco de Mahón con jamón Ibérico, tomates secos con olivas y albahaca

Fresh Mahón cheese with Iberian ham and dried tomatoes with olives and basil

INGREDIENTS (SERVES 4)
500ml (18fl oz) double cream
250g (9oz) fresh Mahón cheese
5 sheets of leaf gelatine, soaked
200g (7oz) Iberian ham or *serrano* ham, sliced very thinly

FOR THE DRIED TOMATOES
10 tomatoes
dash of extra-virgin olive oil
dash of Sherry wine vinegar
salt to taste
pinch of sugar

FOR THE OLIVE AND BASIL OIL
200g (7oz) black olives
1 bunch of fresh basil
250ml (9fl oz) olive oil

GARNISH
pitted black olives, sliced
fresh basil leaves

Pour the cream into a saucepan and bring to the boil. Remove the orange rind from the cheese, cut into small cubes and stir into the hot cream. Return to the boil, take off the heat and add the gelatine, stirring until the leaves dissolve.

Blend the mixture in a food processor and then strain through a sieve into a bowl. Leave to cool, before putting in the refrigerator for 6 hours to set. Then grate the creamy cheese block and set aside.

For the dried tomatoes, scald and peel the tomatoes. Cut in half and deseed. Put in a large baking dish and sprinkle over the olive oil, vinegar, salt and sugar. Place in the oven at 110°C (225°F, gas mark ¼) to dry for 3 hours.

For the olive and basil oil, stone the olives and wash the basil. Blend the olives, basil and olive oil in a food processor to form a smooth runny paste.

Arrange 2 heaps of grated cheese on opposite sides of each plate with a pile of ham in between. Place a dried tomato between each pile and drizzle a little olive and basil oil around the plates. Garnish with sliced olives and fresh basil leaves.

WINE TIPS
SPECIAL OCCASION: **Stairway to Heaven, Castell Miquel, Tramuntana-Costa Nord (€€€)**
SUNDAY LUNCH: **Sió, Ribas, Illes Balears (€€)**
EVERYDAY: **Crianza Franca Roja, José L Ferrer, Binissalem (€)**

Sobrassada (Majorcan sausage) has to be *the* taste of Majorca. This cured sausage, made from meat and pork fat, seasoned with paprika, and similar local sausages, such as *longanizas, culanas* and *bisbe,* are practically the only regular source of meat in the Majorcan diet. Dishes of fresh meat are saved for special occasions. Here, *sobrassada* is served in appetizing partnership with fresh prawns and sweet, juicy mangoes.

Broceta de gambas con sobrassada Mallorquina y vinagreta de mangoy

Prawn kebabs with Majorcan sobrassada and mango salsa

INGREDIENTS (SERVES 4)

400g (14oz) *sobrassada* or *chorizo* sausages cut into small cubes

FOR THE KEBABS
20 large raw prawns
olive oil for frying
salt to taste

FOR THE SALSA
2 mangoes, peeled and finely diced
4 shallots, peeled and finely chopped
8 tablespoons sunflower oil
salt to taste

GARNISH
edible flower petals – from marigolds, nasturtiums or roses
4 deep fried red sorrel leaves
4 deep-fried red Swiss chard leaves

Peel and de-vein the prawns, and remove the heads. Thread 5 prawns onto each of 4 skewers and brown in a little olive oil in a frying pan over a medium heat for about 2 minutes, turning once, until pale pink all over. Add a pinch of salt to taste.

For the salsa, mix the mangoes and shallots together thoroughly in a bowl. Stir in the sunflower oil and a pinch of salt. Leave in the refrigerator for 3 hours to let the flavours blend. Then drain off the surplus oil.

In a frying pan, briefly submerge the flower petals and red sorrel and red Swiss chard leaves in hot oil over a high heat until crisp.

Spoon some well-drained mango salsa onto each plate. On one side, place a pile of sausage cubes and on the other, the skewered prawns. Sprinkle a little mango salsa over the top. Garnish with the flower petals and fried leaves.

WINE TIPS
SPECIAL OCCASION: **Miquel Gelabert Selecció Privada, Pla i Llevant (€€€)**
SUNDAY LUNCH: **Can Majoral Galdent Viognier, Pla i Llevant (€€)**
EVERYDAY: **Vinya Son Fangoz, Toni Gelabert, Pla i Llevant (€)**

Throughout the Balearics, the traditional dishes of the islands reflect the influence of various cultures over many centuries. This *cuscussó*, for example, is a dessert with Arabic roots and an age-old Minorcan speciality, which is particularly popular at Christmas time. The recipe makes excellent use of the wonderful crisp almonds, juicy dried fruit and heavenly scented lemons grown on the island.

Cuscussó Menorquín

Almond and lemon-peel cake, Minorca-style

INGREDIENTS (SERVES 4)

500g (1lb 2oz) granulated sugar

200ml (7fl oz) water

150g (5¹/₂oz) lard

1 tablespoon raisins, soaked for 30 minutes in water

¹/₂ teaspoon cinnamon

1 teaspoon finely grated lemon rind

500g (1lb 2oz) dried crusty bread, crushed into fine breadcrumbs

250g (9oz) blanched almonds, finely chopped

2 ready-to-eat dried figs, very finely chopped

2 ready-to-eat dried apricots, very finely chopped

DECORATION

2 tablespoons pine kernels, lightly toasted under the grill

2 tablespoons raisins

Put the sugar in a saucepan and pour in the water. Stir over a low heat with a wooden spoon until the sugar dissolves.

Raise the heat to medium and stir in the lard, raisins, cinnamon and lemon rind.

When the lard has melted, mix in the breadcrumbs, almonds, figs and apricots. Stir over a medium heat for about 5 minutes, then beat vigorously with a wooden spoon, working the mixture until the *cuscussó* is elastic and pliable, with a consistency similar to marzipan. Add more water if necessary.

Pack the *cuscussó* into a shallow rectangular dish, or form into 12 small balls by rolling the mixture between the palms, and set aside to cool. Before serving, turn the *cuscussó* out of the dish and cut into 12 bars.

Put 3 bars or balls of *cuscussó* onto each plate. Decorate with a few pine kernels and raisins over the top.

WINE TIPS

SPECIAL OCCASION: **Palo de Mallorca (€€€)**

SUNDAY LUNCH: **Can Rich Dulce, Ibiza/Eivissa (€€)**

EVERYDAY: **Original Muscat, Miquel Oliver, Pla i Llevant (€)**

Wines of Baleares

The first DO, Binissalem-Mallorca, was created in Majorca in 1991 and in the early days, bodegas concentrated on local grapes: Manto Negro and Callet for reds, Moll for whites. Since then experiments with Cabernet Sauvignon, Merlot, Syrah and Chardonnay have changed the face of island viticulture. Binissalem is a fairly tightly concentrated area in the centre of the island, and it was joined by a second DO area called Pla i Llevant de Mallorca (literally 'plain and east coast of Majorca') in 2001. This effectively covers the south-eastern half of the island. The result has been quite a spectacular improvement in the island's wines.

DO BINISSALEM-MALLORCA

This is the heart of Majorca's winemaking area. Manto Negro grapes for red wines and Moll (also known as Prensal) for whites are still an important part of the mix, but international varieties are now present in most vineyards.

DO PLA I LLEVANT DE MALLORCA

A very large area, not all of which is under vine. Although the local grapes are cultivated, there is also a great deal of experimentation with international varieties. Quality is generally very high.

OTHER WINES

VdlT Illes Balears A region-wide country wine allowing winemakers more flexibility in what they produce. These range from the everyday to some quite spectacular wines made by bodegas that simply refuse to conform.

VdlT Tramuntana-Costa Nord The north-west half of Majorca, with vineyards running up to the northern mountain range. In this way the whole of the island is covered by a DO or VdlT wine classification.

VdlT Ibiza and VdlT Isla de Menorca Recent island-wide classifications. Some potential, but most of the wine goes into the local tourist trade.

OTHER DRINKS

Palo de Mallorca is an old-fashioned local liqueur made by infusing grape spirit with quinine, gentian, sugar and caramel. The result is dark, almost black in colour with flavours of liquorice and caramel, and a slightly bitter finish. It is usually drunk as a *digestivo*.

Main Bodegas
(listed in alphabetical order), PRODUCER NAME; town/village; web/E-mail address; best wines (r = red, w = white, p = pink) A star (*) indicates particularly good quality.

DO BINISSALEM-MALLORCA
www.binissalemdo.com

JAUME DE PUNTIRÓ; Santa María del Camí; www.vinsjaumedepuntiro.com; Buc (r), JP (r)*

JOSÉ L FERRER; Binissalem; www.vinosferrer.com; Veritas (w), José Ferrer (r), D2UES (r)*

MACIÀ BATLE; Santa María del Camí; www.maciabatle.com; Pagos de María (r)*

DO PLA I LLEVANT DE MALLORCA
www.plaillevantmallorca.es

MIQUEL GELABERT; Manacor; www.vinsmiquelgelabert.com; Chardonnay (w)*, Gran Vinya Son Caules (r)*

MIQUEL OLIVER; Petra; www.miqueloliver.com; Ses Ferritges (r), Aía (r)*

PERE SEDA; Manacor; www.pereseda.com; Pere Seda (r, w, p), Gvivm (r)*

TONI GELABERT; Manacor; www.vinstonigelabert.com; Chardonnay (w)*, Vinyes Velles (r)*

VdIT ILLES BALEARS

ÀN NEGRA; Felanitx; anegra@hotmail.com; Àn (r)*

RIBAS; Consell; www.bodegasribas.com; Sió (r)*

VdIT TRAMUNTANA-COSTA NORD

CASTELL MIQUEL; Alaró; www.castellmiquel.es; Stairway to Heaven (r)*

Canarias (The Canary Islands) are an archipelago of seven islands formed from dormant or extinct volcanoes, approximately 110km (68 miles) east of the north African coast. Under the 1978 Spanish constitution, Canarias became an *autonomía* in its own right, divided into two provinces: Santa Cruz de Tenerife, which includes the islands of Tenerife, La Gomera, El Hierro and La Palma; and Las Palmas de Gran Canaria, which includes the islands of Lanzarote, Fuerteventura, and Gran Canaria. All the islands produce some wine, with the exception of Fuerteventura, and the main industries are tourism, construction and agriculture in approximately equal thirds. Perhaps the most beguiling island is Lanzarote, where in 1730 a

Canarias

volcanic eruption covered the island in lava, which solidified to produce black soil, black landscapes and even black sand on the beaches.

Historically, the islands have been important as a strategic base in the Atlantic Ocean, especially during the exploration of the New World as a supplies stop for ships on their way to South America. They prospered greatly, especially during the boom in the market for *sack*, the sweet, fortified wine based on the styles of wine from Jerez (Sherry) in Andalucía.

LOCAL SPECIALITIES

Fruit and vegetables are the main products of all the islands, and Canarias potatoes (known locally as *papas*) were always the harbinger of summer in northern Europe when they arrived in the spring. Canarias tomatoes have always been a major winter crop and Canarias onions are still an important part of the agricultural economy. Probably the biggest fruit crop is bananas, and the island of La Palma seems to be an endless carpet of velvet-green banana palms. Local restaurants have an infinite number of ways of doing different things with bananas on their dessert menus.

Each island has its own cheeses, but two have made their mark nationally: *queso majorero* is made on Fuerteventura from goat's milk with a little sheep's milk. It's a semi-hard cheese and comes 'fresh' (softer) or *semicurado* (harder). *Queso Palmero* is made from the milk of the long-horned goats of La Palma and is lightly smoked and soft to the touch. There's also a local bread called *gofio*, which is traditionally made from wheat flour, barley, maize or chickpeas, which are roasted and then mixed with water or milk to form a kind of paste that can be baked to taste. Sometimes vegetables (particularly pulses) may be added to the mix.

Canarias boasts tropical temperatures that are ideal for growing more exotic fruits than in the rest of Spain, including avocados, papayas, mangoes, guavas, pineapples and bananas. These feature regularly in the islands' cuisine, enlivened with aromatic herbs and spices. This recipe for *vieja*, a sea fish with a coarse scaly skin and tender white flesh, combines the best of the local produce in an original way.

Vieja a la parilla con crema de papaya y cilantro

Grilled fish with papaya cream and fresh coriander

INGREDIENTS (SERVES 4)

4 *viejas*, or sea bream, each
    weighing about 700g (1lb 9oz)
olive oil
salt to taste

FOR THE SAUCE

100g (3½oz) papayas, peeled and
    roughly chopped
125g (4½oz) caster sugar
juice of 1 lemon
50g (1¾oz) fresh coriander
150ml (5fl oz) double cream
2 eggs

GARNISH

purple basil or coriander
    (optional)
edible flower petals – nasturtium,
    marigold or rose (optional)
balls scooped from melon and
    mango (optional)

Clean and fillet the fish, removing all the bones.

For the sauce, blend the papayas with 75g (2¾oz) of the sugar and the lemon juice in a food processor. Strain the purée through a sieve into a bowl and set aside in the refrigerator.

Blanch the coriander in a saucepan of boiling water. Then blend the coriander and cooking water together in a food processor. Set aside.

Make a custard by heating the cream to boiling point. Then remove from the heat and set aside to cool slightly. Beat the eggs and the remaining sugar together in a bowl. When the cream is warm rather than hot, whisk in the egg and sugar mixture. Return the saucepan to the heat and stir continuously with a wooden spoon over a low heat until the custard thickens. Then stir in the coriander juice and set aside to cool.

When the coriander custard is cool, stir in the papaya purée with a spatula.

Brush the fish fillets with olive oil and season with a little salt. Put the fish under a medium grill and cook for about 5 minutes on each side until golden.

Spoon some papaya and coriander sauce onto each plate, and then put a piece of fish on top. Drizzle over a few drops of olive oil. Garnish with a sprig of purple basil or coriander, a sprinkling of edible flower petals and a few melon and mango balls, if desired.

WINE TIPS

SPECIAL OCCASION: **Brumas de Ayosa Brut Nature (sparkling), Comarcal, Valle de Güímar (€€€)**
SUNDAY LUNCH: **Viñátigo Gual Blanco, Ycoden-Daute-Isora (€€)**
EVERYDAY: **Gran Tehyda Blanco, Valleoro, Valle de la Orotava (€)**

The *papas* (potatoes) of the Canarias are small and sweet, and the mainstay of the islands' economy and cuisine. Today many varieties are cultivated and any of them can be used to create this fragrant, spicy dish. The name comes from the way the potato skins wrinkle up when cooked in salty water – originally in sea water – and from its *mojo* (sauce) of chilli peppers and cumin seeds.

Papas arrugadas con mojo picón
Wrinkled potatoes with a spicy cumin sauce

INGREDIENTS (SERVES 4)

1kg (2lb 4oz) Canarias potatoes or
    small new potatoes (the thicker
    the skins, the better)
4 tablespoons salt

FOR THE SPICY SAUCE

2 chilli peppers, deseeded and
    finely chopped
1 garlic clove, peeled and chopped
salt and black pepper to taste
1 tablespoon ground cumin
1 slice crisp fried white bread,
    crusts cut off, chopped into
    small squares
1 teaspoon paprika
225ml (8fl oz) olive oil
4 tablespoons vinegar or to taste

Wash the potatoes, but don't peel them. Tip into a flameproof casserole, cover with cold water and add the salt. Bring to the boil over a high heat, then reduce the heat to low. Cover the casserole with foil, then put the lid on top. Gently boil the potatoes until all the water has evaporated. Keep a close eye on the water level to make sure the potatoes don't burn dry. Remove the lid and foil, and leave the potatoes in the casserole over a low heat until the skins wrinkle and develop a salty crust. Set aside.

To prepare the sauce, place the chillies, garlic, salt, pepper and cumin in a mortar and crush together with a pestle to form a smooth paste. Add the fried bread and continue crushing. Then mix in the paprika and drizzle in the olive oil, little by little as if making mayonnaise, stirring continuously. Then add the vinegar to taste.

Trim an end of each potato to form a flat base and cut a shallow cross in the other end. Squeeze gently below the cuts to open out the top a little and spoon in a teaspoon of spicy sauce. Stand all the potatoes in a serving dish and serve as an accompaniment.

WINE TIPS

SPECIAL OCCASION: Monje Listán Negro, Tacoronte-Acentejo (€€€)
SUNDAY LUNCH: Viña Norte Barrica, Insulares Tenerife, Tacoronte-Acentejo (€€)
EVERYDAY: Hoyo de Mazo Tinto, El Hoyo, La Palma (€)

The *Guanches*, the original inhabitants of the Canarias, had a simple but nutritious diet based on a mixture of stone-ground and toasted cereals called *gofio*. This coarse flour has survived, pretty much unchanged, to the present day. This thick porridge-like soup, which can be eaten for breakfast, is a fine example of the numerous sweet and savoury recipes that feature the delicious, characteristic flavour of *gofio*.

Sopa de gofio
Roasted corn, wheat and rye soup

INGREDIENTS (SERVES 4)
125ml (4fl oz) olive oil
1 onion, finely chopped
6 tablespoons *gofio*: a coarse flour
    of ground, roasted maize, rye
    and wheat grains
salt to taste
herb oil, to garnish (optional)

Heat the olive oil in a frying pan over a medium heat. Tip in the onion and sauté until transparent. Add the *gofio* and stir with a wooden spoon to form a smooth toasted paste.

Boil a kettle. When the water is hot but not boiling, slowly start adding tablespoonsful to the frying pan, until the ball of *gofio* becomes a smooth runny porridge. Season with a little salt and simmer over a low heat until thickened.

Spoon some *gofio* soup into each bowl. Garnish with few drops of herb oil, if desired.

WINE TIPS

SPECIAL OCCASION: **El Grifo Malvasía Fermentado en Barrica, Lanzarote (€€€)**
SUNDAY LUNCH: **Viñátigo Marmajuela Blanco, Ycoden-Daute-Isora (€€)**
EVERYDAY: **El Lomo Blanco, Tacoronte-Acentejo (€)**

Malvasía grapes make one of the most prized wines of the Canarias, 'Canary Sack'. As a regular consumer of the divine nectar, Robert Louis Stevenson may well have been referring to Canary Sack when he wrote *'Wine is bottled poetry.'* Today, a strong, sweet Malvasía wine is perfect for revitalizing *bienmesabe*: a traditional paste of dried fruits, nuts and egg, similar to marzipan.

Bienmesabe con velo de chocolate blanco y granizado de vino de Malvasía

Egg, almond and sugar paste with a white chocolate crust and Malvasía ice

INGREDIENTS (SERVES 4)

FOR THE *BIENMESABE*
100ml (3¹/2fl oz) mineral water
40g (1¹/2oz) caster sugar
250g (9oz) blanched almonds,
    toasted and finely chopped
125ml (4fl oz) sweet Malvasía
    wine
4 egg yolks, whisked in
    2 tablespoons of milk
finely grated rind of 1 lemon
1 teaspoon ground cinnamon

FOR THE CRUST
125g (4¹/2oz) white chocolate,
    broken into small pieces

FOR THE ICED DRINK
250ml (9fl oz) sweet Malvasía wine

DECORATION
150ml (5fl oz) Pedro Ximénez
    dessert wine, reduced to
    2 tablespoonsful (optional)

Prepare a light syrup by warming the water and sugar in a saucepan over a low heat, stirring carefully until the sugar dissolves. Then add the almonds, stirring continuously with a wooden spoon over a low heat for about 10 minutes. Add the wine, the eggy milk, lemon rind and cinnamon. Continue to stir continuously until a smooth paste forms. Set aside to cool.

For the white chocolate crust, melt the chocolate pieces in a bowl over a saucepan of simmering water. Spread the melted chocolate over a piece of baking parchment lining a baking tray with a palette knife or spatula to create a very thin, even sheet of white chocolate. Briefly chill in the refrigerator until barely hard, then stamp out discs with a round, 6cm (2½in), straight-edged biscuit cutter.

For the iced drink, pour the wine into a saucepan and heat over a medium heat until reduced by half in volume. Pour into a plastic container and set aside to cool before putting in the freezer to ice up.

Spoon some of the iced Malvasía wine into 4 glasses. Place a spoonful of the *bienmesabe* on top, then position a white chocolate disc on top of that. Decorate with the reduction of PX (Pedro Ximénez) dessert wine drizzled over the top (optional).

WINE TIPS
SPECIAL OCCASION: Malvasía Dulce, El Grifo, Lanzarote (€€€)
SUNDAY LUNCH: Humboldt, Insulares Tenerife, Tacoronte-Acentejo (€€)
EVERYDAY: El Grifo Canari Malvasía, Lanzarote (€)

Wines of Canarias

The Canarias have no fewer than 11 *denominación* wines spread over six of the seven islands. The range is wide, and the sweet, fortified wines known in Shakespeare's time as 'Canary Sack' are still made from Malvasía, Pedro Ximénez and Moscatel grapes, particularly on Lanzarote. Main red varieties are Listán Negro and Negramoll. Most interesting, perhaps, are some ancient varieties, long forgotten on the mainland, which still survive on the islands. They include Burrablanca, Breval, Diego, Almuñeco, Sabro, Gual Bermejuela, Forastera Blanca and Vijariego, but the more serious areas are also planting Tempranillo, Cabernet Sauvignon and Merlot. Styles tend to be light and fresh, made for early drinking and largely directed at the tourist trade. Few bodegas have the capacity to export as far as the Iberian peninsula (1,150km/715 miles) let alone to the international market. For general information, see www.bodegacanaria.com.

DO AREAS ON TENERIFE

DO Abona This area occupies the southern quarter of the island, centred around the town of Arico, with vineyards as high as 900m (2,953ft) towards the volcanic crater. They grow most of the island's varieties and make young wines for the tourist trade.

DO Tacoronte-Acentejo On the island's northern tip, this is one area that is able to export and has the quality wines with which to do it: mainly reds from Listán Negro and sweet whites from Malvasía.

DO Valle de Güímar A small area around the town of Güímar on the east coast of the island, with vineyards planted at up to 1,500m (4,921ft). Mainly white-wine grapes (Listán Banco) with some red from Listán Negro.

DO Valle de la Orotava Another small area, directly opposite Valle de Güímar on the west side of the island, making mainly fruity white wines from Listán, Gual and Vijariego.

DO Ycoden-Daute-Isora On the south-western tip of the island, this area is perhaps most famous for the dragon tree of Icod, which is at least 1,000 years old and possibly more.

Wines are largely white, both sweet (Malvasía, Moscatel) and dry (native Canarias varieties).

DO AREAS ON GRAN CANARIA

DO Monte Lentiscal Very small area around Santa Brígida, in the north-east of the island. The best wines tend to be reds made from Listán Negro from the highest vineyards; up to 800m (2,625ft).

DO Gran Canaria A more recent DO (2000) that takes in all the rest of the island apart from Monte Lentiscal. Mostly light, fruity reds from Listán Negro for immediate drinking, and largely sold into the tourist industry.

ISLAND-WIDE DOs

DO Lanzarote Vineyards here are excavated from black volcanic soil and protected from the prevailing winds by walls that have been built around individual vines. Small-scale at present, but makes some of the best traditional Canarias sweet wines from Malvasía.

DO La Palma This beautiful island makes all kinds of wine, but mainly sweet whites in the traditional Canarias style, from Malvasía grapes. There is some good red from Negramoll.

DO La Gomera The most recent DO (2004) in the islands, making mainly light, fresh, young wines, principally warm, fleshy whites from the Forastera grape.

DO El Hierro Makes mainly sweet whites from Moscatel and Pedro Ximénez.

OTHER WINES

The smoky, misty, subtropical north highlands of the island of La Palma make wines called *Vino de Tea*, which don't have a DO but do have a big local following. *Tea* in this instance is the Spanish word for a type of pine from which vats and barrels are made, adding a certain piquancy to the flavour. The wines are then aged for many years in caves excavated in the mountainsides until they oxidize and turn almost black: a style known on mainland Spain as *rancio* (literally 'rancid'). It's not exactly a commercial product, but people who like this sort of thing usually find that it's something they enjoy... mainly on La Palma.

Main Bodegas

(listed in alphabetical order), PRODUCER NAME; town/village; web/E-mail address; best wines (r = red, w = white, p = pink) A star (*) indicates particularly good quality.

DO ABONA
crdoabona@worldonline.es

CUMBRES DE ABONA; Arico; cumbresabona@wanadoo.es; Cumbres de Abona (r, w, p)

DO TACORONTE-ACENTEJO

www.tacovin.com

EL LOMO; Tegueste; www.bodegaellomo.com; El Lomo (r, w)

INSULARES TENERIFE; Tacoronte; www.bodegasinsularestenerife.es; Viña Norte (r)

MONJE; El Sauzal; www.bodegasmonje.com; Monje (r)

DO VALLE DE GÜÍMAR
www.vinosvalleguimar.com

COMARCAL VALLE DE GÜÍMAR; Arafo; www.bodegacomarcalguimar.com; Brumas de Ayosa (r, w, p)

DO VALLE DE LA OROTAVA
www.dovalleorotava.com

VALLEORO; La Orotava; www.bodegavalleoro.com; Gran Tehyda (r, w)

DO YCODEN-DAUTE-ISORA

www.ycoden.com

VIÑA DONIA; Miradero y Ancón Icod; www.bodegasinsularestenerife; El Ancón (r)

VIÑÁTIGO; La Guancha; www.vinatigo.com; Viñátigo (r, w)

DO MONTE LENTISCAL
montelentiscal@telefonica.net

DO GRAN CANARIA
crdogc@terra.es

DO LANZAROTE
www.dolanzarote.com

EL GRIFO; San Bartolomé de Lanzarote; www.elgrifo.com; El Grifo (w)*

DO LA PALMA
www.malvasiadelapalma.com

EL HOYO; Villa de Mazo; www.bodegaselhoyo.com; Hoyo de Mazo (r, w)

DO LA GOMERA
www.fundacionalhondiga.org/crgomera.php

DO EL HIERRO
www.elhierro.tv/crdo

Cantabria is one of the most beautiful parts of Spain, with green landscapes, a craggy coastline, some of Europe's cleanest beaches and a large slice of the breathtaking Picos de Europa. The capital is Santander, a major port during the exploration of the New World, and today still a centre for shipping, trade and car ferries. It's an *autonomía* consisting of a single province: one of the most prosperous in the north of Spain, and one of the leading consumers of wines from elsewhere in the country, although it has no classified vineyards of its own.

The city suffered a massive fire and gale-force winds in a storm in 1941, which destroyed much of its ancient architecture – including the splendid Romanesque

Cantabria

cathedral (only the crypt remains) – as the fire burned for two days. There were, fortunately, very few fatalities, but thousands of families were left homeless, and much of the modern city dates from the 1950s onwards. As one of the most northerly cities of Spain, it remains a popular destination for Spanish people escaping the summer heat of the south.

LOCAL SPECIALITIES

Understandably, with a coastline along the Bay of Biscay, the local gastronomy relies heavily on fish – particularly monkfish, sea bass, sole and turbot, but also sardines, anchovies, mackerel and tuna, along with squid, often served up as a fish stew with potatoes. Shellfish, including *percebes* (goose foot barnacles; *see* Galicia, page 118) and everything from shrimp to lobster, spiny crab to clams can be found in seafront restaurants along the coast.

This lush green landscape is also cattle country, however, and *carne de Cantabria* (Cantabrian beef) is one of the great specialities of the region. The cattle breeds are Alpine Brown, Tudanca and Monchina, bred and raised in the highland pastures, and slaughtered and butchered in the highlands.

There are three protected cheeses from Cantabria. *Picón bejes-tresviso* is a blue cheese from the Liébana region, south-east of the Picos de Europa national park. It's made mainly with cow's milk, but is often blended with some sheep's and goat's milk, depending on what style the cheesemaker wants: creamy or sharper. *Quesucos de liébana* is a white version of the same cheese from the same area, slightly softer and occasionally smoked. *Queso de Cantabria* is a generic cheese made all over the province from cow's milk. It's soft and creamy when young, harder and sharper when mature.

Although Cantabria is better known for its exceptional seafood, the region also produces simple, honest dishes featuring more humble ingredients. One speciality from the coastal area of Laredo is *respigos* (turnip leaves), which are much admired for their slightly hot, peppery flavour. When cooked well, they can accompany any dish, however grand, although pairing the greens with crispy bacon works beautifully.

Respigos de carbón con panceta de cerdo

Sweet chargrilled spring greens with bacon

INGREDIENTS (SERVES 4)

500g (1lb 2oz) piece of streaky bacon
2 leeks, roughly chopped
1 onion, roughly chopped
3 carrots, roughly chopped
1 garlic clove
3 handfuls *respigos* (turnip greens) or other spring greens
salt to taste
olive oil, for deep-frying

GARNISH

sea salt flakes (optional)
sprouting seeds (optional)

Place the bacon, vegetables (except the greens), and garlic in a large saucepan. Cover with cold water and put a lid over the top. Bring to the boil over a high heat and leave to simmer over a low heat for at least 6 hours, to produce a flavoursome stock for a sauce.

While the bacon is cooking, wash the greens well. Bring plenty of water to the boil over a high heat in a large saucepan. Plunge the greens into the water and boil for about 15 minutes. Carefully pour off the boiling water and rinse the leaves under cold running water to cool them down quickly. Lay individual leaves on the grill over the heat of a charcoal barbecue and season with a little salt. (The greens can be finished off under the grill, but never seem to taste quite as good.)

When the bacon is cooked through, remove from the saucepan and cut the piece into 4 cubes. Deep-fry each cube in plenty of olive oil until crispy.

Meanwhile, blend the stock and vegetables together in a food processor. Strain through a sieve to create a smooth sauce.

Pour a little sauce into each dish, then put a cube of the fried bacon on top and arrange a portion of the greens alongside. Garnish the bacon with a few flakes of sea salt and a handful of sprouting seeds, if desired.

WINE TIPS

SPECIAL OCCASION: **Áster reserva, Ribera del Duero (€€€)**
SUNDAY LUNCH: **Valdelosfrailes Prestigio, Cigales (€€)**
EVERYDAY: **Altos de Tamarón, Pagos del Rey, Ribera del Duero (€)**

Cantabria is the most important anchovy-canning region in Spain. During the canning process, the fish are cleaned, salted and preserved. The salty little fillets that emerge from the can are invaluable for creating numerous snacks, appetizers, seafood tapas and sauces. Because it's always so useful to have a supply of anchovies to hand, this recipe demonstrates how straightforward it is to prepare and preserve the fresh fish.

Anchoas en conserva

Preserved north-coast anchovies

INGREDIENTS (SERVES 4)
1kg (2lb 4oz) fresh anchovies
plenty of coarse sea salt
oregano, to taste
paprika, to taste
ground black pepper
100g (3¹/₂oz) caster sugar
extra-virgin olive oil

Clean the anchovies well, removing the heads and guts. It's a delicate task, because the fish should be handled as little as possible, and then only with cold hands. Slit down the back of each fish, separating and boning the fillets, and set aside. (Alternatively, ask a fishmonger to do this.)

Combine the rest of the ingredients, except the olive oil, to make the seasoning. Place a layer of the sweet, spiced salt in the bottom of a large shallow dish. Then arrange a layer of the fish on top and finish with another layer of seasoning.

Leave the dish in the refrigerator for about 2 hours, then transfer the anchovies to a large glass jar, or plastic container, and cover in extra-virgin olive oil. Keep the fish under oil in the refrigerator for up to 3 months.

Every time you want to use the anchovies, wash the fillets well to remove the seasoning and revive with a drizzle of fresh olive oil.

WINE TIPS
SPECIAL OCCASION: Quinta Apolonia Verdejo, Belondrade, Castilla y León (€€€)
SUNDAY LUNCH: LB Gewurztraminer, Luna Beberide, Castilla y León (€€)
EVERYDAY: Txacoli Eizaguirre, Getariako Txakolina (€)

Like many popular recipes in Cantabria and the Basque country, the identity of exactly who first thought of cooking *jibiones* (squid) in their own ink is lost in the mists of time. This dramatic dish of rice cooked in a dark, aromatic sauce, served with squid and mushrooms, is an exciting blend of flavours from land and sea, and certainly rates highly among the great culinary delicacies of northern Spain.

Jibiones asados con arroz negro y boletus
Barbecued Basque squid with black rice and ceps

INGREDIENTS (SERVES 4)

4 *jibiones* (squid), cleaned and
  dried

FOR THE RICE

350g (12oz) short-grain rice
  (*calasparra* and *arborio* are
  suitable)
700ml (1¼ pint) fish stock
2 bags squid ink
splash of single cream

FOR THE CEPS

2 large fresh ceps, sliced
extra-virgin olive oil

GARNISH

olive oil
chives

Cook the rice in a large saucepan with 500ml (18fl oz) of the fish stock and all the ink for about 10 minutes until half-cooked. Transfer the rice to another saucepan, pour in the remaining 200ml (7fl oz) of fish stock, bring to the boil and cook for about 6 minutes. At the end of cooking, stir in a little cream to sweeten the rice.

Preheat the oven to 60°C (140°F). Arrange the mushroom slices on a baking tray, drizzle over some olive oil and roast in the oven for 25 minutes until soft.

Preheat the oven to 180°C (350°F, gas mark 4). Brown the squid under a medium grill for 15 minutes, then transfer to a baking tray and finish cooking in the oven for 3 minutes.

Spoon a little black rice into each bowl, then lay 2 or 3 slices of mushroom on the rice, and balance a roasted squid on top. Garnish with a drizzle of olive oil and 2 chives.

WINE TIPS

SPECIAL OCCASION: Naiades, Naia, Rueda (€€€)
SUNDAY LUNCH: Palacio de Bornos Vendimia Seleccionada Sauvignon, Rueda (€€)
EVERYDAY: Quinto Hinojal, Casto Pequeño, Castilla y León (€)

Blue cheese is a staple of the northern Spanish diet. In Tresviso, *picón* cheese is produced to an ancient formula, which is closely guarded by the local shepherds. Made with sheep's milk for creaminess, cow's milk to support the blue veining and goat's milk for its strong taste, the flavour and intensity of *picón* are unforgettable. In this recipe, the cheese is just one of several distinguished Cantabrian flavours used.

Emulsión de alubias rojas con buñuelo de queso Picón y lomo de boquerón macerado en especias

Creamed kidney beans with blue-cheese fritters and spiced anchovy fillets

INGREDIENTS (SERVES 4)

200g (7oz) fresh anchovies

1 teaspoon salt

1/2 teaspoon each of ground black pepper, ground white pepper, dried oregano, dried thyme and dried rosemary

2 bay leaves

100ml (31/2fl oz) olive oil

11/2 tablespoons wine vinegar

FOR THE KIDNEY BEANS

300g (101/2oz) red kidney beans

1 onion

1 garlic clove

2 teaspoons cayenne pepper

olive oil

salt to taste

FOR THE FRITTERS

100g (31/2oz) *picón*, or blue cheese

200g (7oz) plain flour

2 tablespoons beer

salt to taste

olive oil, for batter and for drizzling

Clean and fillet the anchovies (*see* page 66). Plunge the fillets into cold water, drain and dry well on kitchen paper. Arrange in a single layer in a shallow dish. Combine the salt, peppers, herbs, olive oil and vinegar to make a marinade for the anchovies, and pour over the fish. Place in the refrigerator for 24 hours. Rinse and dry each fillet before serving.

Soak the kidney beans in plenty of cold water overnight.

Bring a large saucepan of water to the boil. Drain the soaked kidney beans, tip into the boiling water and add the onion, garlic and cayenne. Bring back to the boil, then cook over a high heat for 15 minutes. Turn the heat down to medium and continue boiling for at least another 45 minutes, or until the beans are soft. Then drain and put the bean mixture in a food processor and blend until creamy. Pour in as much olive oil as needed to loosen the consistency. Add salt to taste.

For the fritters, mould the cheese into 12 small balls and set aside in the refrigerator. Mix together the flour, beer, a little salt and enough oil to make a thick batter. Roll the balls of cheese in the batter and fry in lots of hot olive oil. Carefully remove from the oil with a slotted spoon, then drain on some kitchen paper.

Spoon some red kidney bean purée onto each plate. Arrange 3 cheese fritters on top and some anchovies on the side. Garnish with a drizzle of olive oil.

WINE TIPS

SPECIAL OCCASION: **Luna Beberide Reserva, Castilla y León (€€€)**

SUNDAY LUNCH: **Vagal Pago de Ardalejos, Castilla y León (€€)**

EVERYDAY: **Casar de Burbia Tinto, Bierzo (€)**

Wines of Cantabria

There are no classified wines in Cantabria, but the Liébana region (of cheese fame; *see* page 62) makes a modest local wine. There are fewer than 50 hectares under vine, mostly divided into small plots, many of them domestic in size and ambition. They grow Mencía and Tempranillo for red wines, Palomino and Verdejo for whites, and total production might peak at 250,000 bottles per year, a good deal of which may be sold off for distillation into *orujo* (*see* below).

CANTABRIA BODEGAS

There are a few small bodegas that have ambitions to win promotion to vino de la tierra status, but commercial production would initially be very small, in the region of just 60,000 bottles per year. There is an even smaller industry for the production of sweet wines made from dried grapes (with thereby concentrated sugars), fermented for two weeks in oak vats. They are known generically as tostadillos.

There is also an unofficial classification for wines of the 'Costa de Cantabria'. Some nine hectares produce about 40,000 bottles a year of white wines made from Albariño, Hondarribi Zuri, Godello, Riesling and Chardonnay. None of these wines has any official status or is seen outside the region.

OTHER DRINKS

Although winemaking is on a very small scale, there is an equally small distilling industry making *orujo de Cantabria*. However, the issue is rather fudged as there is no *denominación*, and pomace from neighbouring regions can be imported for distillation in Cantabria. Some spirits are infused with honey or herbs to make a sweet liqueur. None of these drinks have any official classification as yet.

Along with its neighbours Asturias to the west and the Basque Country to the east, Cantabria has a cider industry, although it isn't as well developed on an industrial scale. Most production is on a domestic level, but there's a good deal of tradition and there is a *cofradía de la sidra de Cantabria* ('Cantabrian cider brotherhood'), which holds its own cider festivals.

Castilla y León is Spain's largest region, with nine provinces: Ávila, Burgos, León, Palencia, Salamanca, Segovia, Soria, Valladolid and Zamora. The cities have been variously capitals, seats of government, universities, cathedrals, myths and legends. It is the heartland of Castile, and was the base from which Castilian forces fought the Moors in the 11th century. It's the land of El Cid and Queen Isabella, who married Ferdinand of Aragón to lay the foundations of a united Spain.

LOCAL SPECIALITIES

It's not surprising that Spain's largest region also has the widest variety of local produce: almost everything Spain produces can be found here in one form or another. Beef products include *carne de Ávila, de Cervera y de la Montaña Palentina* (Palencia), *de Morucha de Salamanca, de Pinares-El Valle* (Soria and Burgos), *ternera de Aliste* (Zamora), *del Bierzo* (León) and *ternera charra* (Salamanca), all farmed in the

Castilla y León

rural pastures of their various provinces. Lamb is important, too: *lechazo de Castilla y León* is milk-fed lamb from all over the region, with a particular speciality being *lechazo Montañas del Teleno* from León. Pork products range from the *cochinillo de Segovia* and *jamón guijuelo* (Salamanca), as well as *embutidos* (sausages), especially *chorizo de Cantimpalos* (Segovia), *morcilla de Burgos, botillos del Bierzo* and *cecina de León*: air-, sun- or smoke-dried sausage.

Cheeses include *queso Castellano*, a hard variety with a nutty flavour which is made all over the region except the province of Zamora, which has its own *queso Zamorano*. Burgos also has its own cheese, softer than Castellano, and usually eaten young and fresh. All these are made with cow's milk. Other cheeses include *queso de Villalón* (Valladolid), which is a sheep's milk cheese, and *queso de Valdeón* (León), a strong blue cheese made from cow's and goat's milk.

Fruit and vegetables are equally varied: León has the *Manzana Reineta del Bierzo*, a special variety of apple that comes in both green and russet. Pulses are widespread: *garbanzos* (chickpeas) *de Fuentesaúco* come from Zamora and *judías del Barco de Ávila* and *alubias de la Bañeza-León* are white and coloured beans; lentils, too – *lentejas de la Armuña* (Salamanca) and *lentejas pardina de Tierra de Campos* are grown in the northern part of the region. Peppers are grown in León; the *pimiento asado del Bierzo* has been around since the 1650s, and *pimientos Fresno-Benavente* are red peppers grown in León and Palencia.

Spanish sausages are famous for their variety and quantity, and one of the most valued is the *botillo* of León. In many ways it is a typical sausage, made of pig's ribs and tail, seasoned with salt, paprika and garlic, smoked and dried, but its size is not typical – it usually weighs about 1.5kg (3lb 5oz). This large sausage makes numerous traditional dishes in this region – hearty, simple and nourishing.

Botillo Leonés

Round pork sausage with cabbage and potatoes

INGREDIENTS (SERVES 4)
1 *botillo*, weighing 1kg (2lb 4oz)
800g (1lb 12oz) green cabbage
salt to taste
800g (1lb 12oz) potatoes
deep-fried sorrel leaves, to garnish
   (optional)

Put the *botillo* in a saucepan and cover with water. Bring to the boil over a high heat, cover with a lid, then cook over a medium heat for about 1 hour until tender.

Wash and shred the cabbage, and add to the saucepan. Add a little salt, bring back to the boil over a high heat, then simmer over a low heat for about 30 minutes.

Peel the potatoes and cut into large, irregular pieces. Add to the saucepan and cook over a medium heat for about 20 minutes until well cooked.

Cut up the *botillo* and serve in bowls, accompanied by the cabbage, potatoes and cooking liquid. Garnish with deep-fried sorrel leaves, if desired.

WINE TIPS

SPECIAL OCCASION: **San Román, Maurodós, Toro (€€€)**
SUNDAY LUNCH: **Pago de Ardalejos, Vagal, Castilla y León (€€)**
EVERYDAY: **Peregrino Tinto, Gordonzello, León (€)**

The farming region of Salamanca is famous for its pastures and chanfaina is a lamb stew that, like paella, has many variations in style and ingredients. The essential ingredient is lamb and the dish traditionally includes all parts of the animal. The dish originates from shepherds, who would make good use of the less attractive parts of the animal in order to prepare this stew. This version of the dish uses only lambs' feet.

Chanfaina

Lamb stew with bay leaves, garlic, hot pepper and white wine

INGREDIENTS (SERVES 4)

8 lambs' feet

2 tablespoons olive oil

1 onion, halved and sliced

3 garlic cloves

2 bunches of parsley

1 clove

pinch of nutmeg

1 teaspoon salt

3/4 tablespoon freshly ground
     black pepper

1 tablespoon plain flour

GARNISH

2 red peppers, roasted

2 eggs, hard-boiled and sliced

Carefully clean the lambs' feet and put in a large saucepan. Cover with cold water and bring to the boil over a high heat, then cook over a medium heat for 1 hour. From time to time, skim off any residue that rises to the surface.

Heat the olive oil in a frying pan and sauté the onion for 10 minutes. Grind the garlic, parsley, clove, nutmeg, salt and pepper to a paste in a mortar with a pestle. Stir into the frying pan with a wooden spoon.

Transfer the meat from the saucepan to a flameproof casserole, saving the meat stock to use later. Tip in the contents of the frying pan. Sprinkle the flour over the meat, onion and seasonings, and stir in some of the reserved meat stock. Simmer over a low heat for 2 hours, until the meat is tender.

Serve the stew in bowls, garnished with roasted peppers and hard-boiled eggs.

WINE TIPS

SPECIAL OCCASION: **Aalto, Ribera del Duero (€€€)**

SUNDAY LUNCH: **Arzuaga Crianza, Arzuaga Navarro, Ribera del Duero (€€)**

EVERYDAY: **La Legua, Emeterio Fernández, Cigales (€)**

Scented, thick and firm, the fresh mushrooms used in this recipe are from the *boletus* family and are a celebration for the taste buds. Here they provide the ideal ingredient when accompanied by a good duck's liver, with a red wine sauce. They are a typical delicacy in autumn, when you can eat them fresh.

Tarrina de boletus y foie macerado en vino tinto

Terrine of ceps and duck's liver marinated in red wine

INGREDIENTS (SERVES 4)

500g (1lb 2oz) ceps (mushrooms), sliced

salt to taste

olive oil, for drizzling

8 sheets of leaf gelatine, soaked in cold water

350g (12oz) fresh duck's liver

2 litres (3¹/₂ pints) red wine

1 tablespoon caster sugar

Preheat the oven to 110°C (225°F, gas mark ¹/₄). Spread the mushrooms on a baking tray, sprinkle on some salt and a drizzle of olive oil. Roast the mushrooms in the oven for 30 minutes. Drain any liquid from the mushrooms into a bowl and, while still warm, stir in the gelatine until dissolved. Add the mushrooms to the liquid and spoon into 4 silicon muffin moulds or 4 compartments of a non-stick muffin tray, to make tub-shaped mushroom jellies. Set aside to cool before leaving in the refrigerator overnight.

Cover the duck's liver with 600ml (1 pint) red wine and marinate for 24 hours. Drain off the wine and brown the liver under a medium grill until cooked through.

Pour the remaining wine into a saucepan and add the sugar. Heat gently over a medium heat, stirring until the sugar dissolves. Then boil to reduce the wine until there is about 150ml (5fl oz) left in the saucepan.

Unmould the mushroom jellies and put one on each plate. Place some duck's liver beside the mushrooms and pour over the wine reduction.

WINE TIPS

SPECIAL OCCASION: **Pintia, Toro (€€€)**
SUNDAY LUNCH: **Dominio de Tares Cepas Viejas, Bierzo (€€)**
EVERYDAY: **Altos de Tamarón, Pagos del Rey, Ribera del Duero (€)**

These sweet handmade spheres, yellow in colour and with the texture of a melting and delicate egg yolk, are an example of how a few ingredients can produce a sublime dessert. Some say they are of Arab origin, although they owe their popularity to the Order of the Carmelites and to one of their most famous nuns, St Teresa of Jesus. With the saffron cream and almond crust of this recipe, they are irresistible.

Yemas de Santa Teresa sobre cremoso de azafrán y crujiente de almendra

Sweet egg yolks with saffron cream and almond crust

INGREDIENTS (SERVES 4)

FOR THE DOUGH
250g (9oz) granulated sugar
250ml (9fl oz) boiling water
11 egg yolks, plus 1 whole egg
grated rind of 1 lemon
55g (2oz) caster sugar
55g (2oz) icing sugar

FOR THE SAFFRON CREAM
2 eggs
30g (1oz) granulated sugar
100ml (3½ fl oz) double cream
pinch of saffron
60g (2¼oz) butter

FOR THE ALMOND CRUST
115g (4oz) granulated sugar
125ml (4fl oz) boiling water
200g (7oz) ground almonds

DECORATION
1 tablespoon icing sugar

For the dough, put the granulated sugar and water in a saucepan and cook, stirring, over a low heat until the sugar dissolves to make a syrup. Leave to cool for 10 minutes. Then beat the egg yolks, one at a time, into the syrup, finally adding the whole egg and lemon rind. Return to the heat and cook gently, stirring constantly with a wooden spoon, until the yolks set.

Sprinkle the caster sugar onto a work surface and pour out resulting dough on top. Leave to cool and then form the dough into small balls between your palms. Roll the balls in the icing sugar and set aside for serving.

For the saffron cream, mix the eggs and sugar together. Add the cream and the saffron and boil in a pan, stirring well so that it does not stick. Then remove from the heat and add the butter, before straining through a fine sieve. Leave to cool and set aside for serving.

For the almond crust, preheat the oven to 180°C (350°F, gas mark 4). Put the sugar in a bowl, pour over the water and stir until the sugar has dissolved. Set aside to cool. Then beat in the ground almonds. Line a baking tray with baking parchment and spread the sweet almond paste thinly over the tray. Bake in the oven for 5 minutes, then remove and pat out the crust by hand. Set aside to cool.

Spoon some saffron cream onto each plate and arrange 3 dough balls on top. Lay a piece of the almond crust beside the balls. Decorate with a dusting of icing sugar.

WINE TIPS

SPECIAL OCCASION: **Flor del Saúco Ora Pro Nobis, Vega Saúco, Toro (€€€)**
SUNDAY LUNCH: **Bornos Sauvignon Dulce, Castilla La Vieja, Rueda (€€)**
EVERYDAY: **Castel Ámbar, Castelo de Medina, Rueda (€)**

Wines of Castilla y León

Castilla y León has an enviable reputation for quality wines, largely due to the success of the Ribera del Duero DO and the Tinto Fino grape (also known as Tinto del País: it's actually the local variant of Tempranillo). Although the wine-producing areas tend to follow the course of the River Duero as it wends its way towards the Portuguese border, there are highland vineyards here up to 900m (2,953ft), with well-drained soils, high in chalk content and ideal for growing vines. At altitude, the sun is hot in the ripening season but the temperature drop at night can be as much as 15 degrees, allowing the vine to 'sleep' rather than continue using up nutrients in the soil needed by the grape during the day. The only white wine of note is made in Rueda from Verdejo and, latterly, Sauvignon Blanc, a contender (along with the Albariño of Rías Baixas; *see* Galicia, page 126) for the title of 'classic white wine of Spain'.

Castilla y León is also the first region to implement the new (2003) VCPRD category. The letters stand for *Vinos de Calidad Producido en Regiones Determinadas* – 'quality wines produced in specific regions' – the EU-wide classification for quality wines.

DO BIERZO
In the province of León, this is the home of the 'difficult' Mencía grape, which had too much acidity until it was tamed by Álvaro Palacios at Corullón. Since then (1999) investment has flooded into Bierzo, which is now making some wonderful wines.

DO CIGALES
Cigales is north of the city of Valladolid, and is a region well known for making rosado (rosé) wines, even though reds are its best, mainly Tempranillo. Soils are well drained with large stones, and the potential is excellent.

DO RIBERA DEL DUERO
The DO that started Castilla y León on the quality trail. Although the region's oldest bodega (Vega Sicilia) dates back to 1864, it was 1982 before the DO was granted, and it was Alejandro Fernández of Pesquera who lit the flame with his 1986 vintage. The main grape is Tinto Fino, the style is concentrated, powerful and perfumed.

DO RUEDA
Historically, Rueda made fortified, Sherry-type wines because the local Verdejo grape oxidized so quickly that unfortified wines were stale before they got into the bottle. Francisco Hurtado de Amezaga of Marqués de Riscal (Rioja) discovered that, when handled properly, Verdejo could produce wonderful, fresh, crisp, clean white wines. Today, they pick at night and transport the grapes under inert gas to protect them from air. Riscal also introduced Sauvignon Blanc into the region. Red wines were admitted in 2001, but whites still dominate.

DO TORO
Toro has a reputation for big, blockbusting reds made from Tinto de Toro (Tempranillo). The land is hot and high, up to 850m (2,789ft), and grapes ripen comfortably without fear of damage by frosts.

VCPRD WINES
Five regions were all promoted from *Vino de la Tierra* to quality-wine status in 2005.

VCPRD Arlanza This straddles the border between Palencia and Burgos and is mainly planted with Tinto del País, Mencía, Garnacha and Cabernet Sauvignon, with Viura and Albillo for whites, though most production is of red.

VCPRD Arribes This follows the course of the River Duero southwards on the western edge of the provinces of Zamora and Salamanca. They grow the local Juan García and Rufete, as well as Tempranillo and Garnacha.

VCRPD Tieras de León In the south of the province of León they grow the local Prieto Picudo grape along with Mencía and Tempranillo for mainly red-wine production. There is some Palomino and Verdejo for white.

VCRPD Valles de Benavente This area neighbours Tierras de León (*see* above), but across the border in Zamora. They grow the same mix of grapes, although there's more emphasis on Tempranillo for future quality wines.

VRCPD Zamora Quite a large area with some vineyards over the southern border in Salamanca, growing mainly Tempranillo, Garnacha and Cabernet Sauvignon with a small amount of white-wine grapes. Once again, reds are better – quite surprisingly good in some cases.

OTHER WINES
VdlT de Castilla y León Created to give flexibility to winemakers and growers who wanted to plant something a little different. Some of the region's best wines come under this classification.

In addition there are registered VdlT zones in Cebreros (Ávila), Sierra de Salamanca, and Valtiendas (Segovia), but many bodegas are gradually migrating to the VdlT de Castilla y León or one of the VCPRD areas if they meet the criteria.

Main Bodegas
**(listed in alphabetical order), PRODUCER NAME; town/village;
web/E-mail address; best wines (r = red, w = white, p = pink)**
A star (*) indicates particularly good quality.

DO BIERZO
www.crdobierzo.es

CASAR DE BURBIA; Carraceledo; www.casardeburbia.com;
Casar de Burbia (r), Hombros (r)

DESCENDIENTES DE J PALACIOS; Villafranca del Bierzo;
bodega@djpalacios.com; Petalos del Bierzo (r), Corullón (r)*

DOMINIO DE TARES; San Román de Bembibre;
www.dominiodetares.com; Bembimbre (r)*, Tares P3 (r)*

ESTEFANÍA; Ponferrada; www.tilenus.com; Tilenus (r), Pagos
de Posada (r)*

PEIQUE; Valtuille de Abajo; www.bodegaspeique.com;
Peique (r)

PRADA A TOPE; Cacabelos; www.pradaatope.es; Palacio de
Canedo (r)

DO CIGALES
www.do-cigales.es

CÉSAR PRÍNCIPE; Fuensaldaña; 983-583-242; César Príncipe (r)*

EMETERIO FERNÁNDEZ; Fuensaldaña; www.lalegua.com; La
Legua (r), La Legua Capricho (r)*

LEZCANO-LACALLE; Trigueros del Valle;
www.bodegaslezcano.com; Lezcano-Lacalle (r)

VALDELOSFRAILES; Cubillas Santa Marta;
www.matarromera.es; Valdelosfrailes (r, p)

DO RIBERA DEL DUERO
www.riberadelduero.es

AALTO; Roa de Duero; www.aalto.es; Aalto (r)*, Aalto PS (r)*

ALEJANDRO FERNÁNDEZ; Pesquera;
www.grupopesquera.com; Alenza (r)*, Pesquera Janus (r)*

ALIÓN; Padilla de Duero; www.bodegasalion.com; Alión (r)*

DOMINIO DE PINGUS; Quintanilla de Onésimo; 983-680-189;
Flor de Pingus(r)*, Píngus (r)*

EMILIO MORO; Pesquera de Duero; www.emiliomoro.com;
Emilio Moro (r), Malleolus (r)*

MATARROMERA; Valbuena; www.matarromera.es;
Matarromera (r)*

MONASTERIO; Pesquera; www.haciendamonasterio.com;
Hacienda Monasterio Reserva Especial (r)*

PAGOS DEL INFANTE; Quintanilla de Onésimo;
pagosdelinfante@usuarios.retecal.es; Lynus (r)*,
Lynus Aurea (r)*

RENACIMIENTO; Olivares de Duero; www.matarromera.es;
Rento (r)*

RODERO; Pedrosa de Duero; www.bodegasrodero.com;
Carmelo Rodero (r)*, Viñas de Valtarreña (r)*

TELMO RODRÍGUEZ; Logroño; cia@fer.es; Matallana (r)*,
M2 de Matallana (r)*

VEGA SICILIA; Valbuena; www.vega-sicilia.com; Valbuena (r)*,
Unico (r)*

DO RUEDA
www.dorueda.com

AGRÍCOLA CASTELLANA; La Seca;
www.agricolacastellana.com; Azumbre (w)*, Cuatro Rayas (w)

ÁLVAREZ Y DÍEZ; Nava del Rey; Mantel Blanco (w)*

DOS VICTORIAS; San Román de la Hornija;
www.dosvictorias.com; José Pariente (w)*

HERMANOS DEL VILLAR; Rueda; www.orodecastilla.com; Oro
de Castilla Verdejo (w)

J & F LURTON; Santiuste de San Juan Bautista;
www.jflurton.com; Hermanos Lurton (w)*

MARQUÉS DE RISCAL; Rueda; www.marquesderiscal.com;
Marqués de Riscal Verdejo (w)*

NAIA; La Seca; bodegasnaia@terra.es; Naia (w)*

PALACIO DE BORNOS; Rueda; www.palaciodebornos.com;
Palacio de Bornos Verdejo (w)

VEGA DE LA REINA; Rueda; www.vegadelareina.com; Vega de la Reina Verdejo (w)*

VERACRUZ; Pozáldez; b.veracruz@terra.es; Ermita Veracruz (w)*

DO TORO
www.dotoro.es

FARIÑA; Toro; www.bodegasfarina.com; Gran Colegiata (r), Campus (r)*

J & F LURTON; Toro; www.jflurton.com; Campo Elisio (r)*, Toro El Albar (r)*

LIBERALIA ENOLÓGICA; Toro; www.liberalia.es; Liberalia (r), Paciencia de Barnard Magrez (r)*

MAURODÓS; Villaester; www.bodegasmauro.com; San Román (r)*

NUMANTHIA TERMES; Valdefinjas; www.eguren.com; Numanthia (r)*

REJADORADA; Toro; www.rejadorada.com; Sango de Rejadorada (r)*, Rejadorada Roble (r)*

VCPRD ARLANZA

HIJOS DE MAXIMO ORTIZ GONZÁLEZ; Covarrubias; Viña Valdable (r)

LA COLEGIADA; Lerma; www.bodegalacolegiada.com; Lerma (r)

VCPRD ARRIBES

HACIENDAS DURIUS-VALLE; Fermoselle; www.haciendas-espana.com; Durius (r), Durius Magister (r)*

LA SETERA; Fornillos de Fermoselle; www.lasetera.com; La Setera Juan García (r)

VCPRD TIERRAS DE LEÓN

GORDONZELLO; Gordoncillo; www.gordonzello.com; Peregrino (r, w)

VCPRD VALLES DE BENAVENTE

OTERO; Benavente; www.bodegasotero.com; Valleoscuro (r, w, p)

VCPRD ZAMORA

ALIZÁN; Moreleja del Vino; www.alizan.net; Alizán Élite (r)

EL CENIT; Villanueva del Campeán; victore@telefonica.net; Cenit (r)*

VdIT DE CASTILLA Y LEÓN

ABADÍA RETUERTA; Sardón de Duero; www.abadia-retuerta.com; Pago Negralada (r)*, Selección Especial (r)*

BELONDRADE; La Seca; belondrade@vodafone.es; Quinta Apolonia (w)*

DEHFSA DE RUBIALES; Fuentes de Ropel; www.galiciano.com; Polivarietal (r)*, Prieto Picudo (r)

FERNÁNDEZ RIVERA; Vadillo de la Guareña; www.grupopesquera.com; Dehesa la Granja (r)

LEDA VIÑAS VIEJAS; Tudela de Duero; www.bodegasleda.com; Leda Viñas Viejas (r)*

LUNA BEBERIDE; Cacabelos; www.lunabeberide.com; Luna Beberide (r)*

MAURO; Tudela de Duero; www.bodegasmauro.com; Vendimia Seleccionada (r)*, Terreus (r)*

VAGAL; Valtiendas; www.vagal.es; Pago de Ardalejos (r)*

W hen the Moors were driven back to Granada, the forces of Castilla y León (Old Castile) recaptured the vast plains south of Madrid (including La Mancha) and subsequently recolonized them with Castilian people who had been driven out during the Moorish occupation, creating Castilla-La Mancha (New Castile). Land concessions meant that many people took advantage of the opportunity to set up their own smallholdings. After the establishment of Madrid as the national capital by King Felipe II in 1561, there were opportunities for these smallholders to do business. The king built a 200km (124 mile) road from Madrid to Granada, the southern capital, recently vacated by the Moors, to speed the royal mails, troops, churchmen and dignitaries; this passed through the provinces of Toledo and Ciudad Real. In those days the journey would have taken two or three days, so the highly paid government officers needed food, wine and accommodation along the way, and the local farmers grew the food and the grapes, made the oil, wine and the cheese. Perhaps this explains why *queso Manchego* is Spain's most popular cheese, even after five centuries.

Today the *autonomía* of Castilla-La Mancha has five provinces: Toledo and Ciudad Real to the south of Madrid, Albacete to the east, and Cuenca and Guadalajara east of Madrid.

Castilla-La Mancha

LOCAL SPECIALITIES

Queso Manchego is made all over the region from sheep's milk. It comes *fresco*, fresh and soft to the touch; *curado*, a harder version, slightly crumbly; and *viejo*, aged and often marinated in olive oil until it turns nearly black. It's often served with *membrillo*, a quince jelly. Other livestock products include *cordero* (lamb) and *lechal* (milk-fed lamb). The lamb comes from 391 named villages through the five provinces, and the sheep are of the local Manchega breed; everything from feed to environment and even transport is covered by a regulatory body.

In the market gardens, aubergines from Almagro (Ciudad Real), *ajo morado* (purple garlic) from Las Pedroñeras (Cuenca) and melons from La Mancha (Ciudad Real) are all protected, as are olive oil from the mountains of Toledo and the Campo de Montiel (Ciudad Real). In the sweet department, there's honey from La Alcarria (Guadalajara) and marzipan from Toledo. The most expensive product, as ever anywhere in the world, is *azafrán* (saffron) *de la Mancha*, which is harvested in six *comarcas* (counties). Don't even ask the price.

The 16th and 17th centuries were the most creative period in Spanish court cookery. Cervantes and Lope de Vega describe in detail the fabulous dishes produced by marrying new foods from America with native ingredients. Partridge from Toledo played a leading role in royal banquets. This modern interpretation updates the age-old flavours with an earthy taste of mushrooms and the sweetness of plums.

Perdiz a la Toledana en diferentes texturas, con escabeche de hongos y frutas de hueso

Partridge Toledo-style with glazed ceps and plums

INGREDIENTS (SERVES 4)

3 tablespoons olive oil, plus extra
    to coat the ceps
4 partridges, cleaned well
2 onions, finely chopped
4 carrots, cut into sticks
1 garlic clove, chopped
1 bay leaf
500ml (18fl oz) water
500ml (18fl oz) red wine
500ml (18fl oz) white wine
salt and pepper to taste
500g (1lb 2oz) ceps (mushrooms),
    sliced
500g (1lb 2oz) plums, stoned and
    cut into 5mm (1/4in) slices
200ml (7fl oz) water
200g (7oz) sugar

GARNISH

sprigs of fresh rosemary
50g (1¾oz) fresh redcurrants

Heat 3 tablespoons of olive oil in a frying pan over a medium heat. Put the partridges in the frying pan and brown all over, turning halfway through the cooking time. Transfer the birds to a pressure cooker and stew for 40 minutes, or until cooked through.

In the same frying pan brown the onions, carrots and garlic over a low heat for 8 minutes. Then tip the vegetables into the pressure cooker. Toss in the bay leaf and cover the partridges and vegetables with the water, and red and white wine. Add salt and pepper, put on the lid, bring to the boil and cook for 15 minutes.

Preheat the oven to 110°C (225°F, gas mark ¼). Put the ceps in a large bowl, season with salt and pepper, and toss in enough olive oil to coat each slice lightly. Spread out the slices on a baking tray and cook in the oven for 30 minutes.

Meanwhile, to make a syrup for the plums, pour the water and sugar into a saucepan and bring to the boil over a medium heat, stirring constantly until the sugar has dissolved. Raise the heat and boil until the syrup thickens. Add the plums to the syrup and boil for 5 minutes. Remove from the heat and stir in the ceps.

Transfer the partridges to a chopping board and quarter each bird: remove the legs and take the breasts off the bone. To make a sauce, strain some of the cooking juices from the pressure cooker into a saucepan and boil over a medium heat until thickened and glossy.

Spoon some glazed mushrooms and plums onto each plate. Arrange two breasts and legs on top, or sit a whole partridge on the plate. Pour a decorative trail of the sauce around the plate. Garnish with a sprig of fresh rosemary and fresh redcurrants.

WINE TIPS

SPECIAL OCCASION: **Emeritus, Dominio de Valdepusa, DO Pago (€€€)**
SUNDAY LUNCH: **El Vínculo, Alejandro Fernández, La Mancha (€€)**
EVERYDAY: **Vega Moragona Alta Selección, La Magdalena, Ribera del Júcar (€)**

In days gone by, shepherds used to eat a hearty meal like this to keep up their strength while moving their flocks from summer to winter pastures and back again in the spring. This is a lighter version, but it will still warm you up even on the coldest winter days, especially when accompanied by lots of crusty bread and a good Spanish wine.

Gachas manchegas

Almorta flour paste with bacon, garlic and paprika

INGREDIENTS (SERVES 4)

4 large potatoes, chopped

1 onion, finely sliced

1 bay leaf

salt to taste

3 or 4 tablespoons extra-virgin olive oil

4 garlic cloves, chopped

1 tablespoon paprika

2 tablespoons *almorta* flour

8 eggs

truffle oil

200g (7oz) rashers of cured back bacon, rind removed

Put the potatoes, onion, bay leaf and salt into a saucepan and cover with cold water. Place a lid on the saucepan and boil over a high heat for about 20 minutes. Then drain the potatoes and onion, and discard the bay leaf.

Meanwhile, heat 2 tablespoons of the olive oil in a frying pan and fry the garlic until golden. Stir the paprika and *almorta* flour into the olive oil with a wooden spoon and cook until toasted. Set aside.

In a saucepan of gently simmering water, lightly poach 4 of the eggs. Put the poached eggs, the contents of the frying pan and the drained potatoes and onion into a food processor. Blend to a very creamy consistency, adding 1 or 2 tablespoons of extra-virgin olive oil as required. Pour into a saucepan and warm very gently over a low heat until hot, but don't let the potato purée boil.

Separate the remaining 4 eggs, carefully wrapping each yolk individually in a little bag made from cling film. Add a pinch of salt and a few drops of truffle oil to each, then seal with tightly knotted cooking string. Cook in a saucepan of boiling water for about 2½ minutes, then remove the bags from the water and set aside to cool.

Whizz the bacon in a food processor until pulverized.

Arrange a mound of bacon in the base of each soup bowl. Then carefully unwrap a truffle-infused egg yolk and place on top. Pour in the hot creamy potato purée until it covers the bacon and half submerges the yolk, then serve immediately.

WINE TIPS

SPECIAL OCCASION: **Finca Antigua Reserva, La Mancha (€€€)**
SUNDAY LUNCH: **Pago de la Jaraba Crianza, La Mancha (€€)**
EVERYDAY: **Castillo de Almansa, Piqueras, Almansa (€)**

A humble dish of bread cubes or crumbs, *migas* formed the staple diet of the peasants in La Mancha, as well as Andalucía, Extremadura and Navarra. Consequently, it's possible to find recipes calling for such diverse ingredients as herring, eggs, grapes, even pomegranates. This *migas* comes from rural La Mancha and is probably the most authentic. It's quick to prepare and tastes marvellous after a long walk in the fresh air.

Migas del pastor
Pan-fried bread cubes with an assortment of meats

INGREDIENTS (SERVES 4)

1kg (2lb 4oz) day-old bread

salt, to taste

30g (1oz) paprika

5 tablespoons virgin olive oil

1 garlic clove, finely chopped

500g (1lb 2oz) bacon, diced

500g (1lb 2oz) *chorizo* sausages, diced

Cut the bread into 5mm (¼in) cubes and place in a bowl. Toss with the salt and paprika and cover with a damp cloth.

Heat the olive oil in a frying pan and sauté the garlic. When golden, add the bacon, and then the *chorizos*. Once the bacon and *chorizos* are crisp and brown, add the bread cubes and fry, stirring continuously, so that the bread becomes crisp too, but doesn't get greasy.

Put a portion of *migas* on each plate and serve immediately.

WINE TIPS

SPECIAL OCCASION: **Arrayán Premium, Finca La Verdosa, Méntrida (€€€)**
SUNDAY LUNCH: **Ruiz Villanueva Syrah, Bruno Ruiz, Castilla (€€)**
EVERYDAY: **Viña Albali, Félix Solís, Valdepeñas (€)**

A soft paste of almonds and sugar called marzipan was introduced to Spain by the Arabs in the 12th century, and proved particularly popular in Castile, Aragón and Granada. Today, it's still enjoyed in many almond-producing regions and features in many recipes. This light, smooth version is complemented by the freshness of the lemon verbena and a touch of liquorice.

Esponja de mazapán con sorbete de hierba luisa y crujiente de regaliz

Marzipan sponge with lemon verbena sorbet and liquorice crunch

INGREDIENTS (SERVES 4)

FOR THE MARZIPAN SPONGE
300g (10½oz) caster sugar
200g (7oz) ground almonds
2 egg whites
1 egg yolk
500ml (18fl oz) water
6 sheets of leaf gelatine, soaked in
    cold water

FOR THE LEMON VERBENA SORBET
200g (7oz) lemon verbena leaves
250ml (9fl oz) hot water
250g (9oz) caster sugar
8g (¼oz) sorbet stabilizer

FOR THE LIQUORICE CRUNCH
4 egg whites
200g (7oz) icing sugar
75g (2¾oz) butter, creamed with
    1 teaspoon liquorice extract

DECORATION
icing sugar, for dusting (optional)

For the marzipan sponge, mix the caster sugar with the ground almonds in a bowl. Lightly beat the egg whites and yolk together and pour, little by little, into the ground almonds, stirring constantly, to form a paste. Put the almond paste in a saucepan with the water and gelatine. Warm over a low heat for about 10 minutes, stirring all the time, until the gelatine has dissolved in a smooth marzipan 'soup'. Don't let the mixture boil. Pour into a bowl and leave to cool, then put in the refrigerator for about 12 hours to set.

Once cooled, blend the marzipan jelly in a food processor or mixer, then use a whisk to increase its volume and make it lighter. Form the mixture into a cylinder and cut into 4 portions.

For the lemon verbena sorbet, infuse the lemon verbena leaves with the hot water for 2 hours. Then mix the infusion with the sugar and stabilizer. Pour into a plastic container and put in the freezer for about 10 hours.

For the liquorice crunch, preheat the oven to 180°C (350°F, gas mark 4) and line a baking tray with baking parchment. Whisk the egg whites until stiff, then gradually add the sugar to form a meringue. Gently fold the meringue into the liquorice butter until evenly distributed. Then spread the mixture onto the tray and bake in the oven for 5 minutes until brown. Leave to cool for 2 minutes, and while still soft stamp out 4 discs with a biscuit cutter.

Put a piece of the marzipan sponge on one side of each plate and a scoop of the lemon verbena sorbet on the other. Decorate with the liquorice crunch and dust with icing sugar, if desired.

WINE TIPS

SPECIAL OCCASION: **Corte Dulce, Pago del Vicario, Castilla (€€€)**
SUNDAY LUNCH: S & G Dulce Natural Tinto, Vinícola de Castilla, La Mancha (€€)
EVERYDAY: **Viña Albali Dulce, Félix Solís, Valdepeñas (€)**

Oregano
Melva

Los "Huevos Rotos"
Los "Huevos Morcillones"
El Revuelto "Habanero"
Las Tortillas { Triqueros
Habas
Melva
Tac...

Wines of Castilla-La Mancha

Castilla-La Mancha has rocketed from the obscurity of mass-market, low-cost, everyday wines to become one of the most dynamic and exciting regions of Spain. Low land prices attracted investment from the 1980s onward, and these hot, high vineyards (600–700m/1,969–2,297ft) have few problems with insect pests and fungal diseases. They grew a great deal of the white Airén and the red Cencibel (the local name for Tempranillo) and very little else, but this was to change radically. Vinícola de Castilla was the first to invest serious money in the La Mancha DO in the 1970s; after a slow start, others followed. The local government pioneered the region-wide VdlT de Castilla in 1999/2000 and also created the mechanism to establish pago DOs. These are single estates (*pagos*) of international reputation, usually not within mainstream DO areas, which have the right to make wines in their own way. The prime mover in the campaign for these was Carlos Falcó, the Marqués de Griñón, of Dominio de Valdepusa (*see* page 94). To date there are only three DO *pagos* in Spain, all in Castilla-La Mancha, with a possible fourth waiting in the wings (Finca Guijoso, Sánchez Muliterno, *see* page 95). The pago DO concept was enshrined in the new national wine law of 2003.

Castilla-La Mancha also pioneered incremental DO areas within the giant La Mancha DO. After years of debate about whether La Mancha was simply too big, two areas within it that have a reputation for consistently higher-level winemaking were identified, and Ribera del Júcar and Uclés were established in 2001 and 2006, respectively. Bodegas can make wine from certified vineyards under the individual DO names, or blend wines and market them as DO La Mancha.

Today, Castilla-La Mancha makes everything from the humblest everyday wines by the local cooperative to world-class wines from individual estates, with everything in between. It is a veritable winemaking powerhouse, driving quality, individuality and value for money.

DO ALMANSA

This is in Albacete, but almost an enclave within the neighbouring DO Alicante and growing Monastrell grapes like its neighbours to the south in Murcia: Jumilla and Yecla. For several years, just one bodega (*see* page 95) has been carrying the flag for Almansa, and doing it well.

DO DEHESA DEL CARRIZAL (PAGO)

This single estate in the Montes de Toledo (Ciudad Real) became a DO pago in 2006. Marcial Gómez Sequeira grows Cabernet Sauvignon, Merlot and Syrah.

DO DOMINIO DE VALDEPUSA (PAGO)

This is the Marqués de Griñón's estate in the province of Toledo; one of the first to achieve pago status in 2003, growing Cabernet Sauvignon, Syrah and Petit Verdot.

DO FINCA ÉLEZ (PAGO)

This was the other first pago DO, along with Valdepusa, founded by film and theatre director Manuel Manzaneque. His 1,000m (3,281ft) high vineyards in the Sierra de Alcaraz (Albacete) grow Tempranillo, Cabernet Sauvignon, Merlot and Chardonnay.

DO LA MANCHA

Europe's largest delimited quality-wine zone in Ciudad Real, Toledo, Cuenca, Albacete and Guadalajara is back from the dead after years of neglect and now turning out some excellent-value wines from Cencibel, Syrah and Merlot. A number of incremental DO areas have been created within it since 2001 (*see* below).

DO MANCHUELA

Another area bridging the gap between La Mancha, Valencia and Murcia, it achieved DO status in 2000. The main grape is the Bobal (as in Valencia) for red wines. There has been a good deal of investment in new bodegas in recent years, including the single-estate Finca Sandoval, which belongs to Spanish celebrity wine-writer Victor de la Serna.

DO MÉNTRIDA

This is one of those forgotten areas of Spain, even though some of the biggest companies make wine here under the VdlT de Castilla (*see* right). There is potential, and land prices are low, even though it's only 70km (44 miles) from Madrid. There are 38 bodegas, of which 15 still don't bottle wine. Traditional reds are Tempranillo and Garnacha, but Cabernet Sauvignon, Merlot, Syrah and Petit Verdot are making waves.

DO MONDÉJAR

An area east of Madrid and north of La Mancha that still has to reach its potential, most of the wines are *jóvenes* for immediate drinking, made from Macabeo (white) and Tempranillo (red).

DO RIBERA DEL JÚCAR

The first incremental DO to be lifted out of the La Mancha DO, in 2003. Bodegas can make wines under either name, according to the origin of the grapes. Production centres around the village of Pozoamargo, in the east of the province of Cuenca.

DO UCLÉS

This was the second incremental DO to be lifted out of La Mancha, in 2006. As with Ribera del Júcar, bodegas can make wine under either DO, according to the origin of the grapes. Uclés is the centre of the area, in the province of Cuenca, south-east of Madrid.

DO VALDEPEÑAS

One of the early classics in Ciudad Real that really did make something of the Cencibel, traditionally oak-aged, warm and mature, at silly prices. Some of Spain's best-value reds come from here.

OTHER WINES

VdlT de Castilla The first region-wide VdlT zone in Spain, created in 2000 to allow winemakers flexibility in the grapes they grow and the methods they use. Tempranillo, Cabernet Sauvignon, Merlot and Syrah are the main varieties.

There are two other VdlT zones: Gálvez (Toledo), which makes everyday wines from Macabeo, Garnacha, Cencibel and Cabernet Sauvignon; and Pozohondo (Albacete), which does the same, mainly with Monastrell and Airén.

Main Bodegas
(listed in alphabetical order), PRODUCER NAME; town/village;
web/E-mail address; best wines (r = red, w = white)
A star (*) indicates particularly good quality.

DO ALMANSA
PIQUERAS; Almansa; www.bodegaspiqueras.es; Castillo de
Almansa (r, w)

DO DEHESA DEL CARRIZAL (PAGO)
DEHESA DEL CARRIZAL; Retuerta del Bullaque;
wwwdehesadelcarrizal.com; Dehesa del Carrizal (r, w)*

DO DOMINIO DE VALDEPUSA (PAGO)
DOMINIO DE VALDEPUSA; Malpica de Tajo;
www.pagosdefamilia.com; Emeritus (r)*, Summa Varietalis (r)

DO FINCA ÉLEZ (PAGO)
FINCA ÉLEZ; El Bonillo; www.manuelmanzaneque.com;
Manuel Manzaneque (r, w)*

DO LA MANCHA
www.lamanchado.es

ALEJANDRO FERNÁNDEZ; Campo de Criptana;
www.elvinculo.com; El Vínculo (r)

FINCA ANTIGUA; Los Hinosos; www.fincaantigua.com; Finca
Antigua (r), Clavis (r)*

MUÑOZ; Noblejas; vibomu@teleline.es; Blas Muñoz (w)*

VINÍCOLA DE CASTILLA; Manzanares;
www.vinicoladecastilla.com; Castillo de Alhambra (r, w),
Señorío de Guadianeja (r)

DO MANCHUELA
www.do-manchuela.com

FINCA SANDOVAL; Ledaña;
www.grandespagos.com/sandoval.html; Finca Sandoval (r)*

PONCE; Villanueva de la Jara; ponce@iniestahoy.com; Clos
Lojen (r), P.f (r)

DO MÉNTRIDA
www.domentrida.es

FINCA LA VERDOSA; La Verdosa; www.arrayan.es; Arrayán
Premium (r)*

DO MONDÉJAR
crdom@crdomondejar.com

MARISCAL; Mondéjar; www.mariscal.es; Cueva de los Judíos
(r), Tierra Rubio (r)

DO RIBERA DEL JÚCAR
www.vinosriberadeljucar.com

CASA GUALDA; Pozoamargo; www.casagualda.com;
Casagualda (r)

LA MAGDALENA; Casas de Haro; vmoragona@ucaman.es;
Vega Moragona (r)

DO UCLÉS
www.vinosdeucles.com

URIBES MADERO; Huete; www.pagodecalzadilla.net;
Calzadilla (r), Gran Calzadilla (r)*

DO VALDEPEÑAS
www.dovaldepenas.es

DIONISOS; Valdepeñas; www.agrobio-dionisos.com;
Dionisos (r)

FÉLIX SOLÍS; Valdepeñas; www.felixsolis.com; Viña Albali (r)

LOS LLANOS; Valdepeñas; www.gbvinartis.com; Pata Negra (r),
Señorío de los Llanos (r)

MIGUEL CALATAYUD; Valdepeñas; www.vegaval.com;
Vegaval Plata (r)

VdlT DE CASTILLA
ARESAN; Villarobledo; info@bodegasaresan.com; Aresan 9
Meses (r)*

CASA DE LA VIÑA; Alhambra; www.domecqbodegas.com;
Albor (r), Casa de la Viña (r)*

CASTIBLANQUE; Campo de Criptana;
www.bodegascastiblanque.com; Baldor (r)

PAGO DEL VICARIO; Ciudad Real; www.pagodelvicario.com;
50-50 (r), Monagós (r)

SÁNCHEZ MULITERNO; El Bonillo; www.sanchez-
muliterno.com; Vega Guijoso (r), Magnificus (r)*

VALLEGARCÍA; Retuerta del Bullaque; www.vallegarcia.com;
Vallegarcia Viognier (w)*, Syrah (r)*

Cataluña (Catalonia) is a prosperous gastronomic powerhouse, rather like the Basque Country, and it was once part of a much larger empire that stretched, at its peak, as far as possessions in Greece and Turkey. Today it's a 'nation within Spain' consisting of four provinces: Girona, Barcelona, Tarragona and Lérida.

Cataluña is solidly Mediterranean in outlook, gastronomy and wines, with a flourishing independent spirit evident in its art (Picasso, Dalí) and architecture (Gaudí, Puig i Cadafalch) and, indeed, every aspect of cultural life. The city of Barcelona with its grand *ramblas* (boulevards) and bustling lifestyle is one of the most exciting cities in the world, as well as being Spain's largest seaport.

Cataluña

LOCAL SPECIALITIES

Although seafood is the staple, particularly along the coast, Cataluña has a rich farming and produce heritage: beef from the high Pyrenees (*ternera de los Pirineos Catalanes*) and associated dairy products, including the specialist cheese *L'Alt Urgell y La Cerdanya*: mild and creamy, and also butter from the province of Lérida. Poultry and pork are also farmed, particularly in the province of Barcelona, with the *Pollo y Papón del Prat* – special breeds of chicken raised in Baix Llobregat – and *salchichón de Vic*, a spicy sausage from the Plana de Vic: only 28 villages are allowed to produce it. As with every other region, *jamón serrano* (cured ham) is ever-present.

Cataluña is a rich source of fruit and vegetables, with listings for *manzana* (apple) *de Girona*, *clementias* (clementines) *de las tierras del Ebro* (Tarragona), olives, citrus fruit, nuts (including the protected *avellana de Reus* (hazelnuts) in Tarragona), *patata de Prades* (potatoes from Tarragona) and rice, which is grown around the Ebro delta as it flows into the Mediterranean. There are four olive-oil areas: Les Garrigues (Lérida), Siurana, Terra Alta and Baix Ebre Montsià (all in Tarragona). And the region as a whole is famous for its confectionery: *turrón* (nougat), chocolate bonbons, praline and Catalan biscuits known as *panellets* (sweet and savoury) and *neules* (sweet). The *Generalitat de Catalunya* (Catalan government) also awards its own quality marks to various local products, including pork, rabbit, lamb and honey.

They say in Cataluña that the purpose of eating together is to have a conversation: the food simply gives you something to do with your hands while you're talking. Nevertheless, a typical Catalan meal with seafood, fruit, vegetables, meat, olive oil and wine is the very model of the healthy Mediterranean diet.

The entire Spanish Mediterranean coast enjoys numerous variations of this dish. All contain rice and are cooked in a *paellera* (paella pan). To many, the best part of the whole dish is the *socarrat*, the slightly burnt crust on the bottom of the pan. This version makes the most of the excellent seafood caught off the Catalan coast and boasts a sophisticated black colour.

Socarrat de arroz negro con pulpitos

Pan-toasted black rice socarrat and baby octopus

INGREDIENTS (SERVES 4)

3 tablespoons olive oil

1 onion, finely chopped

1 green pepper, finely chopped

fish stock

2 garlic cloves, finely chopped

1 tomato, finely chopped

55g (2oz) monkfish

55g (2oz) hake

30g (1oz) mussels

55g (2oz) prawns

200g (7oz) short-grain rice
   (*calasparra* is the traditional
   paella rice, but *arborio* risotto
   rice produces similar results)

2 bags squid ink

salt and pepper to taste

2 bay leaves

500g (1lb 2oz) baby octopus

GARNISH

1 lemon, cut into 8 wedges

chopped fresh parsley

Heat the olive oil in a *paellera* or a very wide, flat frying pan, and sauté the onion and pepper over a medium heat. Meanwhile, bring the fish stock to the boil and then set aside.

Add the garlic and tomato to the pan, stir for a few seconds, then add all the seafood, except for the baby octopus. Sauté until golden. Before adding the unwashed rice to the pan, measure its volume in a measuring jug. Then tip into the pan and continue to sauté. Pour in the ink and stir until the rice is well dyed.

Pour the hot fish stock into a measuring jug so that its volume is double the measured quantity of rice and stir into the *paellera*. Flavour with salt, pepper and the bay leaves, and leave to cook over a low heat for about 15 minutes, without stirring. Preheat the oven to 180°C (350°F, gas mark 4). Put the *paellera* into the oven for 15 minutes until a crust forms.

Meanwhile, wash the baby octopus and cook under a medium grill for 5 minutes. Arrange the baby octopus evenly around the edge of the *paellera*. Garnish the top of the paella with lemon wedges and chopped parsley.

Place the *paellera* ceremoniously in the centre of the table as a centre piece. From there, serve individual portions, taking care to include a little of each ingredient, including the base, the *socarrat*, which should be crisp and toasted.

WINE TIPS

SPECIAL OCCASION: **Milmanda Chardonnay, Miguel Torres, Conca de Barberà (€€€)**
SUNDAY LUNCH: **Nerola Fermentado en Barrica, Miguel Torres, Catalunya (€€)**
EVERYDAY: **Marfil Pansà Blanca, Alella Vinícola Can Jonc, Alella (€)**

Once tasted, the exquisite flavour of *romescu* is never forgotten. Basically, it's a sauce of crushed dried peppers (from which it gets its name) and varying ingredients that originated in Tarragona, which has transcended its coarse seafaring origins to accompany the most sophisticated recipes. Although the counterpoint to a good cod, in contrast with some pieces of bitter fruits, as proposed here, it is not easily beaten.

Bacalao confitado con romescu y dados de frutas ácidas

Salt cod with romescu sauce and fresh fruit

INGREDIENTS (SERVES 4)

FOR THE SALT COD

1kg (2lb 4oz) salt cod fillets, with skin

olive oil

1 garlic bulb, cloves peeled but not chopped

FOR THE *ROMESCU* SAUCE

250g (9oz) onions

500g (1lb 2oz) tomatoes

1 garlic bulb

3 or 4 dried peppers, soaked for 2–3 hours to soften

30g (1oz) bread

15–20 almonds

250ml (9fl oz) olive oil

100ml (3½fl oz) wine vinegar

salt and black pepper to taste

THE FRUIT

1 orange, peeled and segmented

1 kiwi fruit, peeled and sliced

2 slices of fresh pineapple

Put the salt cod in enough cold water to cover and soak in the refrigerator overnight. Try to change the water 2 or 3 times so that the fish releases as much salt as possible at a cool, constant temperature. Drain and dry the salt cod.

In a deep frying pan, heat plenty of olive oil. When very hot, fry the whole garlic cloves until browned all over, then remove from the frying pan and set aside. Reheat the olive oil and add the salt cod fillets to the frying pan, skin-side down. The oil should cover the cod. Fry over a low heat for about 8 minutes until the cod is cooked, then remove from the pan and set aside. Save some of the olive oil to serve later.

Preheat the oven to 180°C (350°F, gas mark 4). Rub all the solid ingredients for the *romescu* sauce with olive oil, including the dried peppers, and spread out on a baking tray. Roast everything in the oven, remembering to remove each different ingredient when cooked. In particular, keep an eye on the almonds, bread and dried peppers, which burn most easily.

When all the ingredients are roasted, remove from the oven and grind to a paste in a pestle and mortar. Press the paste through a sieve to remove any bits. Mix in the olive oil, vinegar, salt and pepper.

Pour a tablespoon of the olive oil in which the salt cod was cooked onto each warmed plate. Place a piece of salt cod and a tablespoon of the *romescu* sauce next to the oil, with some fruit to one side. Pour the remaining sauce into a bowl and place on the table as an accompaniment.

WINE TIPS

SPECIAL OCCASION: **Closa Battlet Blanc, Ripoll Sins, Priorat (€€€)**
SUNDAY LUNCH: **Vía Edetana Crianza, Edetana, Terra Alta (€€)**
EVERYDAY: **Castell del Remei Blanc Planell, Costers del Segre (€)**

The profusion of fresh vegetables that the Catalans use in their cooking results in some spectacularly colourful and richly flavoured dishes. *Sanfaina*, a chunky ratatouille-type vegetable stew, is a typical example. It's amazing how such a simple local dish can transform a plate of smoked sardines into a culinary delight.

Crujientes de lomo de sardines ahumados con sanfaina guisada

Crunchy smoked sardines with mixed vegetables

INGREDIENTS (SERVES 4)

8 sardines

250g (9oz) smoked salt

1 unsliced loaf of bread

olive oil

1 onion

1 green pepper

1 red pepper

1 aubergine

1 courgette

4 red tomatoes

salt and freshly ground black
    pepper, to taste

GARNISH

bunch of chives, chopped

sprig of marjoram

Clean the sardines, remove the bones and separate the fillets.

Preheat the oven to 170°C (325°F, gas mark 3). Cover the base of a large ovenproof dish with half the smoked salt and place the sardines on top, skin-side down. Cover with the remaining salt and put in the oven for 15 minutes. When the fish are cooked, remove from the salt and set aside.

Reduce the oven temperature to 150°C (300°F, gas mark 2). Carefully cut the bread into very thin slices – it's easier to stand the loaf on end and cut the slices horizontally. Arrange the slices in a single layer on baking trays. Drizzle over a little olive oil and bake in the oven for 10–15 minutes until crisp and golden.

Peel and chop the vegetables into largish pieces. Heat a drizzle of olive oil in a frying pan and lightly sauté the vegetables and tomatoes over a medium heat until tender. Then season with salt and pepper.

Spoon the vegetables into the centre of a serving dish, top with the crisp toast slices and place the sardines over the toast. Garnish with chopped chives and a sprig of marjoram.

WINE TIPS

SPECIAL OCCASION: **Avgvstvs Chardonnay, Puig & Roca, Penedès (€€€)**
SUNDAY LUNCH: **Lanius, Alta Alella, Alella (€€)**
EVERYDAY: **Castillo Perelada Blanc de Blancs, Empordà-Costa Brava (€)**

Wines of Cataluña

Cataluña has 11 DO wine areas and is also the heartland for Cava sparkling wine. Although Cava is made elsewhere in Spain, the Cava DO is dealt with here.

Catalan wine astonishes with its diversity. The three classic white-wine grapes are the Macabeo, Parellada and Xarel-lo, and they're found in all kinds of combinations, especially in Cava, sometimes with an admixture of Chardonnay. The Catalan landscape offers excellent opportunities for vineyards, as the altitude climbs from 200m (656ft) on the coast up to 800m (2,624ft) and more in the highlands. In general, everyday wines for the huge tourist industry are made from grapes grown at lower altitudes. The middle ground (300–600m/984–1,968ft) is where more ambitious wines are made and where many of the grapes for Cava are grown, as well as Tempranillo, Merlot and Cabernet Sauvignon. The highest vineyards offer a cool-climate environment for the finest wines, and Pinot Noir, Sauvignon Blanc and Chardonnay acquit themselves well. The result is a range of wines from world-class, structured reds and delicate, aromatic whites to everyday wines enjoyed in wholesale quantities in the beach-front resorts along the coast.

DO CATALUNYA

An (almost) region-wide classification created in 1999, which covers all existing DOs, giving their winemakers the opportunity to experiment, blend from different areas and use grapes that might not be permitted in their home DOs. It also brought vineyards that were part of former VdlT areas into the DO system. Most producers are also members of other DOs.

DO ALELLA

Immediately north of Barcelona, this small area makes whites that are among Cataluña's best, made mainly from the three main varieties (see above) and also Chardonnay.

DO CONCA DE BARBERÀ

This region is gaining a reputation for everyday white wines made from the three Catalan classic varieties plus Chardonnay. Reds are from Cabernet Sauvignon and Merlot, and there is some Pinot Noir, Tempranillo and Garnacha. The higher vineyards (up to 400m/1,312ft) produce excellent cool-climate wines.

DO COSTERS DEL SEGRE

In the province and around the city of Lleida (Lérida), this area has six subzones spread out rather like a clockface, some as far as 100km (62 miles) away. Ironically, the smallest of these, Raïmat, dominates the DO. It belongs to Cava giant Codorníu, and was the first to make serious, world-class wines here. Since the DO was established with just a few bodegas in 1987, there are now some two dozen at work.

DO EMPORDÀ-COSTA BRAVA

The northernmost DO in Cataluña. They're now making excellent whites from Sauvignon Blanc and Chardonnay, and reds from Tempranillo, Cabernet Sauvignon and Merlot, alongside Garnacha and Cariñena; there's a good deal of experimentation with such as Syrah, Chenin Blanc and even Riesling.

DO MONTSANT

Formerly part of the Tarragona DO. The vineyards are in the foothills of the Priorato DO and the ambition is to make wines close to Priorato quality, but at affordable prices. There has been some considerable success capitalizing on old plantations of Garnacha and Cariñena.

DO PENEDÈS

The DO that put Cataluña on the map. The region has become one of Spain's best known, not just for good-value wines but for some of the country's very finest. Many producers also make sparkling wines under the Cava DO.

DO PLA DE BAGES

Centred around Manresa, this ancient area grows the local Picapoll, Macabeo and Parellada plus Chardonnay for whites, and Tempranillo, Garnacha, Pinot Noir, Cabernet Sauvignon and Merlot for reds.

DOQ PRIORATO

This forgotten mountainside came back to life in the 1990s when visionary winemakers realized that grapes from abandoned ancient Garnacha and Cariñena vines could produce wonderfully characterful and concentrated wine. Since then, Cabernet Sauvignon, Merlot and Syrah have been introduced, usually in minority amounts to lift the aromas of the old-vine wines. These are rare and low-yielding, and this is reflected in the price: there are no ordinary wines in Priorato.

DO TARRAGONA

Light, fresh everyday whites and reds, from Garnacha Blanca, Malvasía, Moscatel and (recently) Chardonnay and Sauvignon Blanc. Reds include Garnacha, Tempranillo and Cabernet Sauvignon. Some traditional sweet wines are still made (usually reds from Garnacha), and communion wine for the church is a major market.

DO TERRA ALTA

Practically unheard-of 10 years ago, this remote part of Tarragona is showing considerable promise, with new producers coaxing excellent wines out of Garnacha and Cariñena, with some help from Cabernet Sauvignon, Merlot and Syrah.

DO CAVA

Cava is sparkling wine made by the traditional method, in the bottle, and also comes from other parts of Spain, but most are Catalan in origin, especially around the town of Sant Sadurní d'Anoia, in the province of Barcelona. Main grapes are the Catalan classics: Parellada, Macabeo and Xarel-lo, but Chardonnay is also used, and some Pinot Noir for pink Cavas.

OTHER WINES/DRINKS

Parts of Cataluña still make the traditional *rancio*, which is allowed to oxidize in loosely stoppered bottles, often in the open air, until it turns brown or even black. Today the wines may be sweet or dry, but all have the characteristic, high-strength burnt flavour beloved of aficionados, and are generally served as a *digestivo*.

The other Catalan classic drink is *ratafía Catalana*, made by adding fresh grape juice to brandy so that the juice doesn't ferment and all the grape-sugars are preserved. Various versions are made, from simple, sweet, after-dinner wines to complex infusions usually aged in oak for three months or more.

Main Bodegas
(listed in alphabetical order), PRODUCER NAME; town/village; web/E-mail address; best wines (r = red, w = white, p = pink) A star (*) indicates particularly good quality.

DO CATALUNYA
www.do-catalunya.com

JEAN LEÓN; Torrelavit; www.jeanleon.com; Terrasola (r, w)*

JOAN SARDÀ; Castellví de la Marca; www.joansarda.com; Feixes del Port (r)

MIGUEL TORRES; Vilafranca del Penendès; www.torres.es; Nerola (r, w)*

DO ALELLA
www.doalella.com

ALELLA VINÍCOLA CAN JONC; Alella; www.alellavinicola.com; Ivori (w), Marfil (w)

ALTA ALELLA; Tiana; www.altaalella.com; Lanius (w)*, Dolç Mataró (sweet r)*

PARXET; Tiana; www.parxet.es; Marqués de Alella (w)

DO CONCA DE BARBERÀ
www.doconcadebarbera.com

ABADÍA DE POBLET; Poblet; www.grupocodorniu.com; Pinot Noir (r)*

CONCAVINS; Barberà de la Conca; www.bodegasconcavins.com; Clos Montblanc (r)

MIGUEL TORRES; Vilafranca del Penedès; www.torres.es; Milmanda (w)*, Grans Muralles (r)*

DO COSTERS DEL SEGRE
www.costersdelsegre.es

CANTONELLA; La Pobla de Cérvoles; www.cervoles.com; Cérvoles (r)*

CASTELL DEL REMEI; Castell del Remei; www.castelldelremei.com; Gotim Bru (r)

RAÏMAT; Raïmat; www.raimat.com; Raïmat (r, w)*

DO EMPORDÀ-COSTA BRAVA
doempcb@teleline.es

CASTILLO PERELADA; Perelada; www.castilloperelada.com; Gran Claustro (r)*, Ex Ex (r)*

ESPELT; Vilajuïga; www.cellerespelt.com; Comabruna (r)*, Airam (sweet r)

PERE GUARDIOLA; Capmany; vins@pereguardiola.com; Floresta (p)*, Clos Foresta (r)

DO MONTSANT
www.domontsant.com

CAPÇANES; Capçanes; www.cellercapcanes.com; Costers del Gravet (r), Cabrida (r)*

EUROPVIN FALSET; Falset; europvin@infonegocio.com; Laurona (r)*, 6 Vinyes de Laurona (r)*

VENUS LA UNIVERSAL; Falset; info@venuslauniversal.com; Dido (r), Venus (r)*

DO PENEDÈS
www.dopenedes.com

GRAMONA; Sant Sadurní d'Anoia; www.gramona.com; Gra a Gra (w)*, Mas Escorpi (w)*

JEAN LEÓN; Torrelavit; www.jeanleon.es; Vinya Gigi (w)*, Vinya Palau (r)

JOAN RAVENTÓS ROSELL; Masquefa; export@raventosrosell.com; Heretat Vall-Ventos (w)*, (r)

MIGUEL TORRES; Vilafranca del Penedès; www.torres.es; Mas la Plana (r)*, Reserva Real (r)*

PARÉS BALTÀ; Pacs del Penedès; www.paresbalta.com; Absis (r)*, Dominio Cusiné (r)*

RAVENTÓS I BLANC; Sant Sadurní d'Anoia; www.raventos.com; La Rosa (p)*, Isabel Negra (r)

DO PLA DE BAGES
www.dopladebages.com

GRAU; Maians; www.vinsgrau.com; Jaume Grau Grau (r, w, p)

MASÍES D'AVINYÓ; Santa María d'Horta d'Avinyo; www.abadal.net; Abadal Chardonnay (w)*, Abadal Selecció (r)*

SOLERGIBERT; Artés; www.cellerssolergibert.com; Conxita Serra (r)*, Enric Solergibert Gran Selecció (r)*

DOQ PRIORATO
www.priorat.org

ÁLVARO PALACIOS; Gratallops; bodega@alvaropalacios.com; Finca Dofi (r)*, L'Ermita (r)*

CLOS FIGUERAS; Gratallops; europvin@infonegocio.com; Font de la Figuera (r)*, Clos Figueres (r)*

CLOS MOGADOR; Gratallops; closmogador@terra.es; Clos Mogador (r)*, Manyetes (r)*

COSTERS DEL SIURANA; Gratallops; www.costersdelsiurana.com; Clos de l'Obac (r)*, Miserere (r)*

SCALA DEI; Scala Dei; www.grupocodorniu.com; Cartoixa (r)*

VALL-LLACH; Porrera; www.vallllach.com; Embruix (r)*, Vall-Llach (r)*

DO TARRAGONA
dotarragona@ctmail.net

DE MULLER; Reus; www.demuller.es; Chardonnay (w)*

J M BACH I FILLS; Vila-Seca; www.closbarenys.com; Clos Barenys

DO TERRA ALTA
www.do-terraalta.com

ALTAVINS; Batea; www.altavins.com; Domus Pensi (r), Tempus (r)

BÀRBARA FORÉS; Gandesa; www.cellerbarbarafores.com; El Quinta (r), Coma d'En Pou (r)*

PIÑOL; Batea; www.vinospinol.com; L'Avi Arrufi (r)*, Mather Teresina (r)*

DO CAVA
www.crcava.es

AGUSTÍ TORELLÓ; Sant Sadurní d'Anoia; www.agustitorellomata.com; Kripta (w)*

ALSINA & SARDÁ; El Pla del Penedès; www.alsinasarda.com; Gran Reserva Especial (w)*, Brut (w)*

CODORNÍU; Sant Sadurní d'Anoia; www.grupocodorniu.com; Anna de Codorníu (w)*, Jaume de Codorníu (w)

FREIXENET; Sant Sadurní d'Anoia; www.freixenet.es; Reserva Real (w)*, Brut Barocco (w)*

GRAMONA; Sant Sadurní d'Anoia; www.gramona.com; Celler Batlle (w)*, Imperial (w)*

RAVENTÓS I BLANC; Sant Sadurní d'Anoia; www.raventos.com; l'Hereu (w)*, Manuel Raventós (w)

Extremadura is an agricultural cornucopia. If you can grow it, it grows here: cork, olives, tobacco, cotton, cereals – and vines, of course. In the livestock department, there are sheep, pigs and goats, and it is rumoured that the fabled spicy *chorizo* sausage and *jamón serrano* both have their origins in this pastoral landscape. Two of Spain's largest provinces, Cáceres in the north and Badajoz in the south reside here. The regional capital is the old Roman city of Mérida, although Badajoz has the largest population. Historically, this has been a relatively poor, sheep-herding area: indeed, they say that sheep still outnumber people in Extremadura.

Extremadura

LOCAL SPECIALITIES

Cheese is an important local product, and arguably Spain's finest cheese, *Torta del Casar*, comes from here. It's made from organic sheep's milk, curdled with cardoon flowers, and salted before being matured into a round, cushion-shaped cheese, eaten by cutting a hole in the top and spooning out the contents. Other cheeses of note include *queso de la serena*, made in a similar fashion from the milk of Merino sheep, but often rather firmer when mature, and *queso ibores*, which is a harder, goat's-milk cheese from Cáceres. Ham is the main classic from these parts, including the *pata negra* (black leg) cured hams known as *jamón Iberico*. The very best is *jamón Ibérico de bellota*, from free-range black pigs that have been fed on acorns in the three months prior to slaughter. *Ternera and cordero de Extremadura* (beef and lamb) are also available, from certified farmers and butchers.

Olive oil has its own *denominaciones*, with specialist production in Monterrubio (Badajoz) of Cornezuelo and Picual olives, and Gata-Hurdes (Cáceres) with the Manzanilla Cacerena variety. Protected fruit and vegetables include the *cereza del Jerte*, cherries from the Jerte Valley in Cáceres, picked by hand and sized, graded and certified by the *consejo regulador*, or regulating body. *Pimentón de la Vera* is the paprika from the Vera Valley in Cáceres. The peppers are smoked and dried after harvesting, and powdered before canning: they come sweet or hot according to taste.

There is a special honey made in Villuercas-Ibores (Cáceres) that comes in different styles, according to whether the pollen used in making it comes from flowers or the trees of the forest.

This is an archetypal Extremeña dish, uniting two great local delicacies on a single plate. The *solomillo* (pork fillet) – and *pata negra*, the region's cured ham – come from the semi-wild black pigs that flourish in the cork-oak forests. *Torta del Casar* is arguably Spain's finest cheese. It's ripened until a lid can be cut in the crusty top and an almost liquid cheese spooned out.

Solomillo de cerdo Ibérico con binomio de queso de torta del casar y verduras escabechadas

Black-pig pork fillet with a duo of Torta del Casar and vegetables

INGREDIENTS (SERVES 4)

500ml (18fl oz) red wine
500ml (18fl oz) white wine
4 garlic cloves, peeled
freshly ground black pepper
800g (1lb 12oz) pork fillet
200g (7oz) *Torta del Casar*,
    or ripe brie, rind removed
100g (3¹/₂oz) carrots
100g (3¹/₂oz) courgettes
100g (3¹/₂oz) celery
100g (3¹/₂oz) aubergine
100g (3¹/₂oz) spring onions
1 leek
250ml (9fl oz) olive oil
2 teaspoons vinegar
1 teaspoon salt
40g (1¹/₂oz) mushrooms
40g (1¹/₂oz) redcurrants
1 teaspoon olive oil
1 teaspoon Sherry vinegar
handful of alfalfa sprouts,
    to garnish

Pour the red and white wines into a large bowl. Add the garlic, black pepper and pork and marinate in the refrigerator for at least 24 hours.

Preheat the oven to 170°C (325°F, gas mark 3) and line a baking tray with baking parchment. Spoon the cheese onto the tray and bake for 5 minutes to form a thin crisp. Remove from the oven and set aside to cool.

Cut the carrots, courgettes, celery, aubergines and spring onions into sticks of equal length. Heat 1 tablespoon of olive oil in a frying pan over a medium heat and sauté each vegetable separately until slightly softened but still crunchy. Cut the leek lengthways into thin strips and blanch for 30 seconds in boiling water until pliable. Put the vegetables into 4 separate bundles and tie together with a strand of leek. In a frying pan, warm the olive oil, vinegar and salt over a low heat for 2 minutes. Set aside to cool, then immerse the vegetable bundles in the salty oil to marinate.

Finely chop the mushrooms and put in a bowl with the redcurrants. Toss with 1 teaspoon of olive oil and 1 teaspoon of Sherry vinegar.

Remove the pork fillets from the marinade, pat dry and place under a hot grill for 10 minutes, turning, until well browned all over. Preheat the oven to 110°C (225°F, gas mark ¹/₄). Transfer the pork fillets to a roasting tray and roast in the oven for 8 minutes, or until cooked through. While still warm, cut the pork into 4 pieces, each about 4cm (1¹/₂in) long.

Place a piece of pork and a vegetable parcel on the plate, spoon a little redcurrant and mushroom salsa onto the side and pour some of the salsa sauce around the base. Garnish with a wafer of crunchy cheese crisp and a handful of alfalfa sprouts.

WINE TIPS

SPECIAL OCCASION: **Tallant de Vega Esteban, Ventura de Vega, Ribera del Guadiana (€€€)**
SUNDAY LUNCH: **Puerta Palma Finca Las Tenderas, Marcelino Díaz, Ribera del Guadiana (€€)**
EVERYDAY: **Celtus, Viña Santa Marina, Extremadura (€)**

In many of the poorer parts of Spain, necessity has always been the mother of invention. For generations, peasants have used their imaginations to create some ingenious, nourishing dishes from the most basic ingredients. In this instance, a tasty but humble dish of egg and onion fritters is elevated to fine-dining status when served with an extravagant sweet-wine sauce.

Repápalos extremeños

Egg and onion fritters with tempura vegetables and a port and red-wine sauce

INGREDIENTS (SERVES 4)

6 eggs, beaten
2 garlic cloves, finely chopped
1 tablespoon chopped fresh parsley
1 teaspoon chopped fresh thyme
salt and pepper to taste
4 thick slices day-old white bread,
   crusts removed, reduced to
   crumbs in a food processor
1 onion, finely chopped
100ml (3¹/₂fl oz) olive oil
200g (7oz) duck's liver
250ml (9fl oz) port
250ml (9fl oz) red wine
250ml (9fl oz) Pedro Ximénez
   dessert wine
250ml (9fl oz) water
2 teaspoons ground black pepper
2 bay leaves
1 tablespoon caster sugar

GARNISH

30g (1oz) plain flour
16 spinach or Swiss chard leaves

Mix the eggs, garlic, parsley, thyme, salt, pepper, breadcrumbs and half the onion together vigorously to form a stiff paste.

Heat 2 tablespoons of the olive oil in a frying pan and sauté the rest of the onion until softened. Purée the liver and onion with a drizzle of port, red wine and Pedro Ximénez in a food processor. Season with salt and pepper. Divide the bread paste into 12 equal pieces and rub each between your palms to shape a medium-sized ball. Poke a finger into each ball and hide a small quantity of liver purée in the centre. Seal up the hole by pinching the sides together and carefully reshaping the ball.

Pour the remaining port and red wine, water, pepper and bay leaves into a saucepan and bring to the boil over a medium heat. Then drop in the bread balls and poach for 10 minutes until slightly puffed-up and firm. Drain well on kitchen paper. Then heat the remaining olive oil in a frying pan over a medium heat, add the bread balls and fry, turning frequently, until golden. Drain on kitchen paper.

Bring the port and wine back to the boil and simmer until thickened to a sauce consistency. Meanwhile, pour the rest of the Pedro Ximénez into a frying pan, stir in the sugar and boil to reduce until syrupy.

Beat the flour with a little iced water to make a light tempura batter. Dip the spinach in the batter so the leaves are only lightly coated. Fry in hot oil until crisp.

Pour 3 pools of port and wine sauce onto each plate. Place a fritter on top of each. Garnish with spinach or Swiss chard leaves and a drizzle of the Pedro Ximénez sauce around the plates.

WINE TIPS

SPECIAL OCCASION: **Corte Real Platinum, Extremeña, Extremadura (€€€)**
SUNDAY LUNCH: **Dominium Merlot, Medina Hermoso, Extremadura (€€)**
EVERYDAY: **Torremayor, Santa Marina, Ribera del Guadiana (€)**

Retinto is a breed of cattle, the finest of Spain's indigenous breeds. They are reared on the lush pastures of Extremadura and Andalucía, and allowed to roam freely over the green grass throughout their lives. The cattle are sent to slaughter when they are about 12 months old. Such special treatment ensures that their meat has a superior flavour, tenderness and succulence, which clearly distinguishes it from all other beef.

Caldereta de añojo retinto con Amanita cesárea confitada, vainilla y flor de huevo

Tender beef casserole with wild mushrooms, sweetened with vanilla

INGREDIENTS (SERVES 4)

4 tablespoons olive oil

900g (2lb) *retinto*, or other
    tender beef, cut into cubes

salt and pepper to taste

5 garlic cloves, chopped

200g (7oz) carrots, cut into sticks

4 leeks, finely sliced

400g (14oz) onions, chopped

4 bay leaves and 2 sprigs of thyme

choricero peppers, ground

100g (3¹/₂oz) flour

500ml (18fl oz) red wine

250ml (9fl oz) beef stock or water

100g (3¹/₂oz) wild mushrooms

1 vanilla pod

1 green pepper, finely chopped

1 red pepper, finely chopped

¹/₂ aubergine, finely chopped

¹/₂ courgette, finely chopped

250ml (9fl oz) Sherry vinegar

GARNISH

500ml (18fl oz) Pedro Ximénez wine

4 eggs (optional)

Heat half the olive oil in a flameproof casserole over a medium heat. Season the beef with salt and pepper, then fry in batches, until browned all over. When the last batch is browned, return all the beef to the casserole and add the garlic, carrots, 2 of the leeks, onions, bay leaves, thyme and *choricero*. Sauté until the onions start browning, then stir in the flour with a wooden spoon and pour in the red wine. Bring to the boil and leave to thicken before stirring in the stock or water. Simmer over a medium heat for about 1 hour, until the meat is tender. Transfer the meat to a saucepan. Strain the sauce through a sieve over the meat and set aside to reheat before serving.

Meanwhile, preheat the oven to 110°C (225°F, gas mark ¹/₄). Spread the mushrooms on a baking tray and drizzle over a little olive oil. Split the vanilla pod, scrape out the seeds and sprinkle onto the mushrooms; cook in the oven for 6 minutes.

In a frying pan, heat the remaining olive oil. Sauté the green and red peppers, aubergine and courgette briefly before pouring in the Sherry vinegar. Continue cooking over a medium heat for about 10 minutes until browned.

Reduce the Pedro Ximénez in a saucepan until syrupy and glossy.

In a frying pan, fry small batches of the remaining leeks in olive oil until crunchy. Drain on kitchen paper.

Spoon some meat with the sauce into the centre of each plate and place some sautéed vegetables and mushrooms alongside. Garnish with a crown of fried leeks and a drizzle of Pedro Ximénez around the edge of the plate. Top everything off with a poached egg, if desired.

WINE TIPS

SPECIAL OCCASION: **Tallant de Vega Esteban, Ventura de Vega, Ribera del Guadiana (€€€)**
SUNDAY LUNCH: **Puerta Palma Finca Las Tenderas, Marcelino Díaz, Ribera del Guadiana (€€)**
EVERYDAY: **Celtus, Viña Santa Marina, Extremadura (€)**

The wild birds and small game that inhabit the beautiful Extremaduran countryside have always played an important part in the local diet. Fresh herbs and marinades are widely used to flavour and tenderize the meat: here, sprigs of fresh rosemary infuse the rabbit with a sweet scent of grassy fields. The asparagus and fruit add a modern flourish to the taste of the dish.

Conejo al romero

Rabbit with fresh rosemary

INGREDIENTS (SERVES 4)

1 rabbit
salt and freshly ground black
      pepper to taste
30g (1oz) fresh rosemary
250ml (9fl oz) extra-virgin
      olive oil
100g (3¹/₂oz) caster sugar
2 teaspoons water

FOR THE SAUCE

30g (1oz) caster sugar
150ml (5fl oz) water
40g (1¹/₂oz) blueberries
200ml (7fl oz) port
200ml (7fl oz) red wine
2 drops rosemary essence
500ml (18fl oz) beef stock

GARNISH

12 asparagus spears, trimmed
3 Golden Delicious apples, peeled
      and cut into sticks
55g (2oz) redcurrants
4 sprigs fresh rosemary

Once the rabbit is clean, remove the head and cut cleanly through the rib cage midway between the fore and hind legs. Then split the joints in half lengthways and separate into 4 pieces, each with a leg and part of the saddle. Then bone out the saddle part. Make a hole in the centre of each saddle flap and push the leg through up to the thigh. Tie the bone and meat together with cooking string.

Preheat the oven to 110°C (225°F, gas mark ¹/₄). Make a straight cut in the lower part of the thigh visible below the flap. Rub salt, pepper and rosemary into the cut. Then rub olive oil all over the legs, place in a roasting tin and roast in the oven for 10 minutes. Then grill the legs until golden brown.

Meanwhile, put the sugar and water into a casserole and heat gently to form a light caramel. Add the fried rabbit to the casserole, cover and cook gently for 45 minutes.

For the sauce, put the sugar and water into a saucepan, bring to the boil over a medium heat, stirring until the sugar is dissolved. Continue boiling to form a light caramel. Then caramelize the blueberries over a low heat for about 15 minutes. Leave to cool, then blend in a food processor and strain the purée through a sieve. Pour the port, wine and 2 drops of rosemary essence into a saucepan, bring to the boil over a medium heat and simmer to reduce by half. Add the beef stock, return to the boil and continue to reduce over a low heat for another 15 minutes.

For the garnish, cook the asparagus in boiling water for 5 minutes. Arrange with the apple on a baking tray. Brush with olive oil and place under a hot grill to brown. Spoon a trail of the sauce down the centre of each plate. Place a portion of rabbit on top. To one side, place 2 sticks of apple and prop up 3 asparagus tips against them. Add a flourish of port and wine sauce and garnish with redcurrants and rosemary.

WINE TIPS

SPECIAL OCCASION: **Puerta Palma Finca El Campillo, Marcelino Díaz, Ribera del Guadiana (€€€)**
SUNDAY LUNCH: **Attelea Crianza, Ruiz Torres, Ribera del Guadiana (€€)**
EVERYDAY: **Privilegio de Romale, Antonio Ortiz Ciprián, Ribera del Guadiana (€)**

Wines of Extremadura

There's only one DO wine in Extremadura: Ribera del Guadiana, named after the vineyards along the valley of the River Guadiana, which flows through Badajoz and, for some of its course, forms the border between Spain and Portugal before flowing into the Atlantic in the Gulf of Cádiz. This is a relatively new DO, created in 1997 from six country-wine areas that had been chipping away at the international market for many years. They became subzones of the DO, still keeping their original names, which may be mentioned on the label: Montánchez (central Cáceres), Cañamero (south-eastern Cáceres), Ribera Baja del Guadiana (western Badajoz), Ribera Alta del Guadiana (eastern Badajoz) and Tierra de Barros (central and south-eastern Badajoz). This last is centred around Almendralejo, and one bodega in particular, Inviosa (now Bodegas Lar de Barros), first cracked the export market to let the world know that Extremadura could make wines at this level. Managing Director Marcelino Díaz created a new boutique bodega to drive the point home.

A wide variety of grapes are grown, including the local Cayetana, Pardina, Borba, Chelva and Montúa for whites, and Garnacha Tintorera and Jaén Tinto for reds. Most wines of export quality will be made mainly from Tempranillo, Cabernet Sauvignon, Graciano, Mazuela, Merlot, Monastrell, Syrah and even a little Pinot Noir.

VdlT EXTREMADURA

Some producers didn't want to join the DO in 1997, and outside investors were attracted by the quality (and low price) of land in Extremadura, so the local government created the *vinos de la tierra* (VdlT) to allow flexibility and a free hand and to encourage inward investment. There are now around eight bodegas working within the VdlT, five of whom are also members of the DO. Tempranillo, Cabernet Sauvignon and Garnacha are the favoured grapes for the (mainly) red wines.

Main Bodegas

(listed in alphabetical order), PRODUCER NAME; town/village; web/E-mail address; best wines (r = red, w = white)
A star (*) indicates particularly good quality.

DO RIBERA DEL GUADIANA
www.riberadelguadiana.org

DOLORES MORENAS; Los Santos de Maimona; www.doloresmorenas.com; Melithon (r), Real Provisión (r)

LAR DE BARROS; Almendralejo; www.lardebarros.com; Lar de Lares (r), Lar de Oro (r)

MARCELINO DÍAZ; Almendralejo; www.madiaz.com; Puerta Palma Finca El Campillo (r)*, Finca Las Tenderas (r)

VdlT EXTREMADURA
LUÍS GURPEGUI MUGA; San Adrian (Navarra); www.gurpegui.es; Gurpegui (r), Pintoresco (r)

MEDINA HERMOSO; Medina de la Torres; www.medina.cc; Dominium (r)

Galicia

This is a beautiful area north of Portugal known as 'Green Spain' for the lushness of its vegetation and its Atlantic weather influences: cool by Spanish standards with magnificent river valleys with steep, craggy banks and almost fjord-like estuaries (*rías*) in the north (*rías altas*) and west (*rías baixas*). The capital is Santiago de Compostela, whose cathedral has been a pilgrimage destination for more than 1,000 years. Galicia's origins are Celtic and Celtic imagery is to be found everywhere.

Galicia has four provinces: A Coruña and Pontevedra along the west coast, and Lugo and Ourense inland. A Coruña is the port from which the Spanish Armada sailed against England in 1588 and it still has a strong maritime tradition.

LOCAL SPECIALITIES

Queso tetilla is a cheese made from cow's-milk, originally from the A Coruña/Pontevedra border, although it is now made throughout the region. *Cebreiro* (cow's milk with a maximum of 40 per cent goat's milk), *San Simón da Costa* (Alpine and Frisian cow's milk) and *arzúa-ulloa* (cow's milk) are all cheeses made in A Coruña and Lugo.

Seafood is the most prevalent dish in every restaurant, although the torrential rivers gushing forth from the coastal crags are breeding-grounds for *lampreas* (lampreys). Other waterborne food includes crab, lobster, crayfish, sea bass and turbot. *Pulpo á la Gallega* (octopus with olive oil and sweet paprika) is widely regarded as the best octopus in Spain; *centollo*, or spiny crab, is another local speciality. The signature dish of the region is, however, *percebes* (goose foot barnacles). An edible member of the barnacle family, they're usually served as a starter with a strong pair of pliers to get them open, with the local Albariño wine. *Mejillones de Galicia* (mussels from the rías) also have their own *denominación*. *Ternera Gallega* is the protected name of meat from the local cattle, and the local cured ham, known as *lacón Galego*, has its own DO.

Patata de Galicia is the *denominación* for potatoes of the Kennebec variety grown in specific areas; another local vegetable is *grelo*, a kind of slightly bitter, spinach-like vegetable sometimes described as turnip tops, and unique to this part of Spain.

The small village of Cea in Ourense produces *pan de Cea*, a bread produced there since medieval times in domed, granite, wood-burning ovens. Finally, *miel de Galicia*, the local honey, comes in various exotic styles, is tightly protected and named according to its delicate nuances: *milflores* (floral), *eucalypto* (eucalyptus), *castaño* (chestnut) and *silva* (woodland).

In Galicia, they eat all manner of seafood and fish, from barnacles and squid to turbot and horse mackerel. Also known as scad, the horse mackerel is one of most popular blue fish in Spain. In this stew, its intense flavour is more than a match for the wine and pepper. Together they represent the essence of the Gallego diet.

Caldero de jurel encebollado con chipirón de anzuelo y caldo corto especiado

Spicy horse-mackerel stew with onion and baby squid

INGREDIENTS (SERVES 4)

FOR THE SPICY FISH STOCK
200g (7oz) fish heads and bones
1 leek, sliced
1 carrot, sliced
1 onion, quartered
ground pepper
100ml (3½fl oz) fruity white wine
1 tablespoon cider vinegar

FOR THE STEW
3 potatoes, peeled and diced
4 medium horse mackerel steaks
salt and pepper
2 tablespoons olive oil
2 onions, sliced
500g (1lb 2oz) baby squid
1 bay leaf

FOR THE SALSA
2 tablespoons olive oil
5 garlic cloves, peeled and crushed
pinch of ground white pepper
1 tablespoon vinegar
1 teaspoon paprika

To make the stock, put all the fish stock ingredients in a large saucepan with 1 litre (1¾ pint) cold water, bring to the boil over a high heat, then reduce the heat to low and simmer for 20 minutes. From time to time, skim off any residue that rises to the surface of the stock.

Strain the stock into another saucepan, add the potatoes and boil gently for about 15 minutes, until nearly cooked. Then season the horse mackerel with salt and pepper. Add to the saucepan and cook for a further 10 minutes. Transfer the potatoes and horse mackerel to a bowl, and set the stock aside.

To make the salsa, heat the olive oil in a frying pan over a low heat. Add the garlic and sauté until golden. Remove from the heat, let the cloves cool a little, then stir in the pepper, vinegar and paprika. Set aside.

To assemble the fish stew, heat the olive oil in a casserole over a low heat and sweat the onions for 5 minutes until softened. Then raise the heat to medium and sauté the baby squid with the onions. When the squid are cooked, add the potatoes, horse mackerel, most of the reserved stock, bay leaf and salsa to the casserole, stirring so that the potatoes break down to thicken the sauce slightly. Simmer over a low heat for 3–4 minutes to let the flavours combine.

Serve a ladleful of the stew in each bowl, garnished with a few pieces of horse mackerel and a bay leaf (optional).

WINE TIPS

SPECIAL OCCASION: **Arautiam, Mar de Frades, Rías Baixas (€€€)**
SUNDAY LUNCH: **Terra Firme, Terra de Cruces, Rías Baixas (€€)**
EVERYDAY: **Pazo de Monterrey, Nuevo Milenio, Monterrei (€)**

No aficionado of northern Spanish cooking could resist the exquisite *empanadas* (pasty-like pies) that are the mainstay of Galician tapas. Maize flour, either on its own or mixed with wheat flour, is used for making the pastry, which gives the pies their golden colour and moreish taste. The *empanadas* are filled with the excellent fresh fish and shellfish that are caught off the coast all year round.

Empanada de sardinas asadas y verduras

Sardine, tomato and red pepper pie

INGREDIENTS (SERVES 4)

FOR THE DOUGH
400g (14oz) wheat flour
400g (14oz) maize flour
pinch of salt
1 sachet easybake yeast
100g (3½oz) lard, at room
    temperature
500ml (18fl oz) lukewarm water
1 egg, beaten

FOR THE FILLING
2 red peppers
250ml (9fl oz) olive oil
3 onions, finely chopped
400g (14oz) tomatoes, peeled,
    deseeded and chopped
pinch of salt
1 bay leaf
1kg (2lb 4oz) fresh sardines,
    cleaned, guts, heads and scales
    removed
1 egg, beaten

Sift the flours onto a clean work surface and stir in the salt and yeast. Push the dry ingredients into a heap and make a well in the centre. Put the lard, half the lukewarm water and the egg into the well and mix together, adding more water as required and kneading vigorously to produce a smooth dough. Transfer to an oiled bowl, cover with a damp cloth and leave in a warm place for about 1 hour to rise.

Preheat the oven to 180°C (350°F, gas mark 4). Rub the peppers with a little olive oil and roast for 25 minutes. When cool, peel and cut the peppers into strips. Then heat 2 tablespoons of the olive oil in a frying pan and sauté the onions over a medium heat for 5 minutes until softened but not browned. Add the pepper strips, tomatoes, salt and bay leaf and simmer for about 10 minutes until thickened.

Meanwhile, remove the bones from the sardines and separate the fillets.

Preheat the oven to 220°C (425°F, gas mark 7). Cut the dough in two, making one piece slightly larger than the other. Sprinkle a little flour over the work surface and roll out the larger piece with a rolling pin. Brush olive oil around the inside of a large ovenproof dish and line with the dough, with a little spilling over the top all the way round. Spread half the pepper and tomato sauce onto the dough, arrange the sardines evenly on top and then spread over the remaining sauce.

Roll out the rest of the dough and lay it over the top of the *empanada*, moistening and sealing the edges with your fingers. Trim to neaten. Prick the surface with a fork and make a small hole in the centre for the steam to escape. Brush the top with beaten egg and bake in the oven for about 40 minutes, until well browned.

Serve the *empanada*, either warm or cold, cut into squares.

WINE TIPS

SPECIAL OCCASION: **Pazo de Señorans Selección de Añada, Rías Baixas (€€€)**
SUNDAY LUNCH: **Valdesil Godello, Valderroa, Valdeorras (€€)**
EVERYDAY: **Gran Reboreda, Campante, Ribeiro (€)**

Galicia is the world's second-largest producer of mussels (after China) so, not surprisingly, mussels are the region's most popular fast-food. This recipe, serving mussels with octopus and potatoes, is a tribute to the familiar, deep-rooted flavours of the area. The local potatoes are called *cachelos* and take their name from the *cachos* (small pieces) they are cut into for cooking.

Ravioli de pulpo con cachelo confitado en pimentón dulce sobre charlota de mejillón

Ravioli of octopus with confit potatoes in sweet paprika on a mussel cake

INGREDIENTS (SERVES 4)

100ml (3½fl oz) olive oil

1 teaspoon paprika or Spanish pimentón

2 *cachelos* (large potatoes), peeled, sliced thinly and cut into 1cm- (½in-) wide strips

salt to taste

1 octopus

½ red pepper, finely diced

½ green pepper, finely diced

½ onion, finely diced

2 gherkins, finely diced

1 tablespoon Sherry vinegar

1 tablespoon olive oil

200ml (7fl oz) dry white wine

24 mussels, washed and debearded

55g (2oz) agar agar

GARNISH

olive oil

seaweed, deep fried (optional)

Heat the olive oil in a frying pan and mix the paprika into hot olive oil with a wooden spoon. Remove from the heat and leave to marinate for a few minutes. Then fry the potatoes in the paprika oil. When cooked and well coloured, remove from the frying pan, sprinkle with a little salt and set aside.

Freeze the octopus tentacles. When well chilled and firm, carefully cut into slices. Lay 2 strips of potato to form a cross. In the centre, place a slice of octopus. Wrap the potato around the octopus to make a ravioli-like parcel. Preheat the oven to 180°C (350°F, gas mark 4). Brush a baking tray with olive oil, arrange the potato raviolis on the tray and place in the oven for about 10 minutes until the octopus is tender and the potato golden.

Mix the peppers, onion and gherkins together, then add the vinegar, olive oil and salt to make a salsa.

Tip the wine and mussels into a casserole, cover and cook over a high heat for about 4 minutes until all the shells have opened. Discard any that don't. Remove the mussels from their shells. Pour 200ml (7fl oz) of the mussel stock into a saucepan and reduce on the stove for 30 minutes. Sprinkle in the agar agar and stir to dissolve and form a jelly. Leave to cool before stirring in most of the salsa (reserving some for a garnish). Set aside.

Line 4 small individual semi-circular moulds with the the mussels. Fill with a small portion of the salsa and cover the top with mussels. Put in the refrigerator until set. Carefully remove the mussel cakes from their moulds. Place one on each plate, accompanied by some octopus 'ravioli'. Garnish with the remaining salsa, a few drops of olive oil and fried seaweed, if desired.

WINE TIPS

SPECIAL OCCASION: **Don Pedro de Soutomaior Neve Carbónica, Galegas, Rías Baixas (€€€)**

SUNDAY LUNCH: **Airón, Alemparte, Ribeiro (€€)**

EVERYDAY: **Viña Godeval, Valdeorras (€)**

This nutritious dish is traditionally made in a three-legged iron *pote* (pot) hanging over an open fire, which is where it gets its name. It belongs to the family of hearty winter stews, which are so characteristic of the Spanish diet. What differentiates this Galician version from those of other regions is that this recipe always includes white string beans, potatoes and pork.

Pote Gallego
Traditional stew, Galicia-style

INGREDIENTS (SERVES 4)
500g (1lb 2oz) dried chickpeas
100g (3½oz) haricot beans
200g (7oz) lamb skirt
150g (5½oz) salt pork
4 pieces of pig's ear
100g (3½oz) ham
250g (9oz) *chorizo* sausages, chopped, plus extra to garnish
4 handfuls of turnip tops, or other green leaves, washed and shredded
1 *hueso de caña* (leg bone of beef)
salt to taste
1 tablespoon olive oil
1 litre (1¾ pint) beef stock
300g (10½oz) potatoes, peeled
fresh parsley, finely chopped, to garnish

The day before making this dish, put the chickpeas and beans into a large saucepan, cover with warm water and set aside to soak overnight. Also put the lamb, salt pork, pig's ear, ham and *chorizos* in a saucepan, cover with cold water and set aside to soak for 24 hours.

In a saucepan of boiling water, blanch the turnip tops with the leg bone, salt and olive oil over a medium heat for 10 minutes, or until tender. When tender, remove from the heat, drain, cool under running cold water and set aside.

In another large saucepan, place the lamb skirt, salt pork, pig's ear, ham and *chorizos*, cover with water, bring to the boil over a high heat, then turn the heat down and simmer over a low heat for 3 hours.

Drain the chickpeas and beans and put in a cloth bag. In a separate saucepan, cook the chickpeas and beans in the beef stock for at least 1 hour until tender.

When the meats are nearly cooked, add the whole potatoes and the turnip tops. Continue to cook for about another 30 minutes over a low heat, until the potatoes are cooked and the meats are cooked through.

Serve the stew in deep bowls. Garnish with a few pieces of *chorizo* and a sprinkling of parsley. Alternatively, serve the meats, and the chickpeas and beans separately.

WINE TIPS

SPECIAL OCCASION: **VX2 Cuvée Caco, María Álvarez Serrano, Ribeiro (€€€)**
SUNDAY LUNCH: **Thémara, Enológica Temera, Ribeira Sacra (€€)**
EVERYDAY: **Terra do Gargalo Tinto, Gargalo, Monterrei (€)**

Wines of Galicia

Galicia has five DO zones and most of the best wines are white to match the local seafood. The most important grape is Albariño and it was this, particularly from the coastal Rías Baixas DO, that first brought fame to the region: the style is crisp, with fresh, peachy fruit and a delicious, lip-smacking finish. On the vine it has strong similarities to the Riesling: legend says that it was originally brought to Galicia by German monks on the pilgrimage trail to Santiago. Godello is the region's second grape: another fresh and crisp white, but with a gentle hint of hazelnuts on the finish. Many Galician wines also have some Treixadura and Loureira, which flourish in the more humid, inland valleys.

Although the red Mencía grape is grown all over the region, Galicia's only serious red wines come from the Ribeira Sacra DO. This is perhaps the most spectacularly beautiful part of the region, and the wines tend to be made by small producers. The style is light, with an smoky perfume and crisp fruit, often aided by a little oak. These wines are enjoyed young and fresh.

DO RIBEIRO
The oldest and biggest area, a continuation inland of Rías Baixas but in Ourense. Here Godello is the chief grape for white wine: lovely fruit but often with a delicious hazelnut finish.

DO VALDEORRAS
The furthest inland. Expect light, fruity reds from Mencía and delicate whites from Godello.

DO RIAS BAIXAS
Mainly along the western coast and the border with Portugal in Pontevedra, but there are some vineyards over the border in A Coruña. The Albariño grape is king here, making lovely, peachy-fruit whites with delicious acidity.

DO RIBEIRA SACRA
Mainly red wines made from Mencía along this beautiful valley in Ourense, which is dotted with ancient monasteries.

The wines range from delicious fruity gluggers to some seriously interesting stuff.

DO MONTERREI
The smallest of all, this is a mainly white-wine area growing Treixadura, Doña Blanca and Godello. Reds are light and made mainly from Mencía and Bastardo.

OTHER WINES
VdIT Betanzos Light, everyday wines, reds from Alicante and Mencía, whites from Palomino and Albariño in the province of A Coruña.

VdIT Val do Miño-Ourense Another area for lightweight, everyday wines: whites from Albariño and Godello, reds from Mencía and Caiño.

OTHER DRINKS
Orujo (www.orujodegalicia.org) is Galicia's 'national' drink. It's a clear spirit distilled from the pomace (grape skins), after the wine has been pressed (as with *marc* in France and *grappa* in Italy), and for some reason the grape-varieties grown in Galicia make a particularly smooth and fragrant spirit, albeit with the bite that comes with any *aguardiente* (*eau de vie*). Galegos drink is as a *digestivo* after a meal, most wineries

produce it and all restaurants stock it. As well as the basic spirit, it's available flavoured with herbs and coffee.

One popular way of enjoying it is the *quemada* (literally 'burnt'): *orujo* is poured into a large earthenware bowl with sugar (115g/4oz for each litre of spirit), orange and lemon peel and coffee beans. Some enthusiasts also add other botanicals and these are stirred in to steep in the liquid. The mixture is then ignited and stirred using a long-handled ladle. Sometimes sugar is burned in the ladle and poured in periodically during the stirring. The heat drives the flavours of the botanicals into the spirit and, when the flames on the surface turn blue, it's ready to drink – after a short period of cooling. The tradition goes back to the 11th century, and the elixir was once believed to have medicinal and even magical properties.

Main Bodegas
(listed in alphabetical order), PRODUCER NAME; town/village; web/E-mail address; best wines (r = red, w = white) A star (*) indicates particularly good quality.

DO RIBEIRO
www.do-ribeiro.com

MARÍA ÁLVAREZ SERRANO; Leiro; www.cotodegomariz.com; Coto de Gomariz (w)*, VX2 Cuvée Caco (r)*

VIÑA MEÍN; Leiro; www.vinamein.com; Viña Meín (w)*, Viña Meín Tinto Clásico (r)

DO VALDEORRAS
www.dovaldeorras.com

DÍA-NOITE; Petín; www.galiciano.com; Galiciano Día (w), Galiciano Noite (r)

SANTA MARTA; Córgovo; santa.marta@teleline.es; Viñaredo Godello (w)*, Viñaredo Mencía (r)

DO RÍAS BAIXAS
www.doriasbaixas.com

AGNUS DEI; Meaño; www.vinumterrae.com; Agnus Dei (w)*

CASTRO MARTÍN; Puxafeita; www.bodegascastromartin.com; Castro Martin (w)*, Avián (w)*, Casal Caeiro (w)*

MARTÍN CÓDAX; Vilariño-Cambados; www.martincodax.com; Organistrum (w)*, Gallaecia (w)*, Martín Códax (w)*

DO RIBEIRA SACRA
www.ribeirasacra.org

MOURE; Saviñao; www.adegasmoure.com; Abadía da Cova (r)*, Abadia da Cova (w)*

RECTORAL DE AMANDI; Amandi; www.bodegasgallegas.com; Rectoral de Amandi (r)

DO MONTERREI
www.crdomonterrei.com

GARGALO; Verín; www.verino.es; Terra do Gargalo (w)*, Terra do Gargolo (r)

I t's ironic that the smallest *autonomía* in Spain (in terms of population) should have the biggest reputation for its wines. A population of about 300,000 (half of whom live in the capital, Logroño) has its own single province, known until 1980 as Logroño, and self-governing as La Rioja since 1982. Previously it was seen as part of Castilla y León (Old Castile) but with strong influences from neighbouring Basque-oriented Navarra and Álava. In the days before roads, the River Ebro, which flows through the north of the region and forms its boundary with the Basque Country and Navarra, was the main means of transportation between the Cantabrian Mountains and the Mediterranean.

La Rioja

Indeed, La Rioja has been one of the major crossroads of Spain since the *camino de Santiago*, the pilgrim route from France to the cathedral in Santiago de Compostela, was established in the 9th century. Pilgrims carrying the staff, scallop and gourd of St James still make the journey: 800km (497 miles) from the French border north of Roncesvalles and 1,500km (932 miles) for the diehards who start their walk in Paris.

LOCAL SPECIALITIES

Although Rioja is famous for its lamb, beef (especially that certified by ASCRIVAC: the Beef and Cattle Breeders' Association of Rioja) and pork (and, inevitably, *jamón serrano*), it's also a rich source of fruit, vegetables and confectionery. The town of Rincón de Soto in the east of the region is famous for its Blanquilla and Conference pears, which have their own DO, and the market-garden cauliflowers from Calahorra and its surrounding villages are protected, as are peppers (*pimiento Riojano*) from the whole region, honey, cheese, wine vinegar, olive oil and preserves and pickles made from horticultural products. Local protection extends to confectionery, biscuits, *fardelejos* (a fried pastry-cake stuffed with marzipan) and the marzipan itself: *mazapán de Soto* from Soto en Cameros.

A typical traditional Riojan meal would, of course, begin with tapas, perhaps followed by *menestras* (a stew of seasonal vegetables, sometimes garnished with ham), then *embutidos*: spicy sausages, typically *chorizo* or *morcilla* (black pudding), often served with stuffed peppers; with a main course of *roast cordero* (lamb) or *cabrito* (kid). That's the simple food of La Rioja, although today there's a very much wider choice.

Using the very finest sausages in this straightforward recipe is the key to its deliciousness. Unlike most stews, which usually improve on reheating, *patatas a la Riojana* is best eaten immediately, so let it rest only briefly after cooking to give the sauce time to thicken.

Patatas a la Riojana
Potatoes cooked Riojan-style

INGREDIENTS (SERVES 4)

1 tablespoon olive oil

3 garlic cloves, chopped

1 onion, finely chopped

1/2 chilli pepper, finely chopped

1 green pepper, chopped

1kg (2lb 4oz) potatoes, peeled
   and roughly chopped

200g (7oz) *chorizos*, sliced

salt and freshly ground black
   pepper to taste

sprig of fresh thyme, to garnish

Heat the olive oil in a flameproof casserole, add the garlic and sauté until golden. Tip in the onion and sweat over a low heat until lightly browned. Then add the peppers. Sauté gently for 10 minutes, before adding the potatoes and *chorizos*. Stir all the ingredients together well and cover with cold water. Bring to the boil over a high heat, reduce to medium and simmer for about 20 minutes until the potatoes are cooked. Season with salt and pepper.

Serve the potatoes and sauce in an earthenware dish, and pile the *chorizos*, peppers and onion on top. Garnish with a sprig of fresh thyme.

WINE TIPS

SPECIAL OCCASION: **Finca Valpiedra, Rioja Alta (€€€)**
SUNDAY LUNCH: **Dominio de Ugarte, Heredad Ugarte, Rioja Alavesa (€€)**
EVERYDAY: **David Moreno Crianza, Rioja Alta (€)**

In Spain, the consumption of asparagus in La Rioja is three times higher than the national average. Not surprisingly, recipes making the most of this distinctively flavoured vegetable abound. In this example, asparagus and green peppers are teamed with hake, a lovely steaky white fish, and served with a traditional regional sauce.

Merluza frita sobre lecho de espárragos y pimientos con emulsión de guiso antiguo

Fried hake on a bed of asparagus and green peppers

INGREDIENTS (SERVES 4)

700g (1lb 9oz) hake fillets, cut
    into 3cm (1¼in) strips
plain flour, lightly seasoned with
    salt and pepper
1 egg, beaten
sunflower oil, for frying
3 tablespoons extra-virgin olive oil
3 green peppers
12 green asparagus spears
3 tablespoons olive oil
1 onion, chopped
1 garlic clove, chopped
1 carrot, chopped
200g (7oz) short-grain rice
1 litre (1¾ pint) chicken stock
salt and pepper to taste
3 spring onions, finely sliced,
    to garnish

Roll the hake strips in the flour, then in the egg. Fry the strips for 60 seconds in a deep-fat fryer or a deep frying pan containing plenty of sunflower oil over a high heat. Drain well on kitchen paper. Transfer to a frying pan and fry over a medium heat for about 5 minutes. Remove from the frying pan and set aside.

Heat the extra-virgin olive oil in a frying pan and fry the whole peppers, turning from time to time, until tender. Cover and set aside to cool, before peeling and cutting into strips.

Trim the asparagus spears and arrange the tips on a baking tray. Brush with olive oil and place under a medium grill for about 5 minutes until tender.

For the sauce, heat the olive oil in a saucepan and sauté the onion and garlic until golden. Then add the carrot and rice and sauté for 2 minutes, before stirring in the chicken stock. Boil over a medium heat for 25 minutes. Season with salt and pepper and mix well. Then push through a sieve to make the sauce.

Place some strips of green pepper on each plate and lay 3 asparagus tips on top. Arrange the pieces of hake on the bed of vegetables. Sprinkle with a little salt and garnish with some slices of spring onion. Serve the sauce separately in a small jug.

WINE TIPS

SPECIAL OCCASION: **Viña Tondonia Gran Reserva Blanco, López de Heredia, Rioja Alta (€€€)**
SUNDAY LUNCH: **Plácet, Palacios Remondo, Rioja Baja (€€)**
EVERYDAY: **Cosme Palacio Blanco Fermentado en Barrica, Palacio, Rioja Alavesa (€)**

Spanish kitchens specialize in serving top quality meat, which literally melts in the mouth, and meat doesn't come much sweeter or more tender than young lamb. This dish is a classic example of how the delicate flavour of the lamb can be enhanced with traditional fresh herbs. The indulgent twist of serving the lamb with truffled bread cubes introduces a modern edge to authentic Spanish fare.

Costillar de cordero lechal confitado en leche de oveja con romero, tomillo y migas trufadas

Marinated rack of young lamb with rosemary, thyme and truffled bread cubes

INGREDIENTS (SERVES 4)

1 loaf of white bread, crusts removed, cut into small cubes

pinch of paprika

salt and pepper to taste

3 tablespoons water

100g (3½oz) streaky bacon rashers, cut into small pieces

1 *chorizo*, 20cm (8in) long, chopped into small cubes

3 garlic cloves, chopped

1 rack of young lamb

1 litre (1¾ pint) sheep's milk

sprigs of fresh thyme

sprigs of fresh rosemary

1 tablespoon olive oil

truffle oil

1 black French truffle, very thinly sliced

sprigs of fresh thyme, to garnish

The night before, tip the bread cubes into a large bowl and sprinkle in the paprika, salt, pepper and water. Toss well, then set aside overnight. Also, put the streaky bacon and *chorizo* in a bowl, mix in the garlic and leave overnight.

Early the next morning, remove the bones from the rack of lamb, making diagonal scores in the fat with a knife. Place the boneless piece of lamb in a roasting tin and cover with the milk, rosemary and thyme. Put in the oven and braise at 50°C (125°F) for 10 hours. At the same time, put the ribs in a roasting tin and roast in the oven for 4 hours until browned.

To make a sauce to serve with the lamb, transfer the bones to a large saucepan, cover with cold water and bring to the boil. Simmer over a low heat for 30 minutes, then strain the stock into a clean saucepan. Continue simmering to reduce and thicken the stock. Season with salt and pepper.

When the lamb is cooked, cut into 4 portions and place each piece under a medium grill for 5 minutes until the fat on top is browned.

Heat the olive oil in a large frying pan or wok over a medium heat. Sauté the bacon, *chorizo* and garlic until the bacon is browned. Then tip the bread cubes into the frying pan. Turn off the heat and toss the bread with the bacon and *chorizo* to absorb all their flavours. Finally, drizzle over a little truffle oil and toss well.

Pile 2 tablespoons of the bacon, *chorizo* and bread on each plate, with a few truffle shavings scattered over the top. Lean a piece of lamb on the pile, then pour a little sauce around the plate. Garnish with sprigs of fresh thyme.

WINE TIPS

SPECIAL OCCASION: **Hiru 3 Racimos, Luís Cañas, Rioja Alavesa (€€€)**
SUNDAY LUNCH: **Allende Tinto, Rioja Alta (€€)**
EVERYDAY: **Dinastía Vivanco Crianza, Rioja Alta (€)**

Swiss chard, artichokes, green beans, peas, asparagus, mushrooms and *borrajas* are all cultivated in abundance in the gardens of La Rioja. Their flavours are so intense and fragrant that they can be used individually as a starter. In this very simple but well-balanced dish, for example, the borage gives the crunchy pork a real boost.

Borrajas salteadas con papada de cerdo

Sautéed borrajas with pork cheeks

INGREDIENTS (SERVES 4)

1kg (2lb 4oz) *borrajas* (a green leafy vegetable with a white stem, similar to Swiss chard), washed and shredded
200g (7oz) pork cheeks
500ml (18fl oz) sunflower oil
salt and pepper to taste
1 tablespoon olive oil
sprigs of fresh parsley, to garnish

Bring a large saucepan of salted water to the boil over a high heat. Drop in the *borrajas* and cook for about 15 minutes until tender. Let the leaves cool in the cooking water.

Meanwhile, preheat the oven to 110°C (225°F, gas mark ¼). Put the pork cheeks into a roasting tin, pour over the sunflower oil and roast in the oven for 4 hours, or until cooked through.

Drain off the oil from the pork. Then brown the pork in a frying pan and cut into cubes.

Drain the *borrajas* well, season with salt and pepper, then drizzle over a little olive oil and toss to distribute evenly.

Place a deep metal ring in the centre of each plate and pack in the *borrajas*. Then arrange the cubes of pork on top. Carefully remove the ring and garnish with sprigs of fresh parsley.

WINE TIPS

SPECIAL OCCASION: **Marqués de la Concordia, Hacienda La Concordia, Rioja Baja (€€€)**
SUNDAY LUNCH: **Valenciso, Rioja Alta (€€)**
EVERYDAY: **Marqués de Cáceres Tinto, Rioja Alta (€)**

Wines of La Rioja

Rioja was the wine that changed Spanish winemaking in the 19th century. The two main pioneers were the Marqués de Murrieta in 1852 and the Marqués de Riscal in 1856, both of whom, quite separately, had lived in Bordeaux and studied the way wine was made there, and brought the technology back to La Rioja. It was a laborious and expensive endeavour, and their neighbours predicted financial disaster; however, fate intervened from the 1870s onward, when the phylloxera vine louse devastated the vineyards of France and French *négociants* came to Rioja in search of wine to sell to their customers. They were delighted to find that 'Bordeaux style' winemaking was turning out something recognizable in Rioja, and the first Rioja boom began. The French vineyards eventually recovered, of course, but the wines of Rioja remain a French favourite, particularly in the south-west.

Although the early pioneers brought Bordeaux vines to go with their Bordeaux technology (some Cabernet Sauvignon and Merlot vines are still found here and there) it was the triumph of the local Tempranillo grape that secured the future of Rioja wine, and it has since gone on to become Spain's flagship grape under various different names. Traditional Riojas use a mix of grapes: Tempranillo for fruit, Mazuelo for tannin and acidity, Graciano for structure and Garnacha for strength and warmth. The right combination of these (every bodega has its own secret formula) makes wines of great finesse, style, elegance and keeping-qualities. These days, however, as the market demands wines for more immediate drinking, there's a trend towards wines with 90 or even 100 per cent Tempranillo, which are drinkable a scant two years after the vintage and, in many cases, offer more of a snapshot of their *terroir* than the classic styles of wine.

In any case, the official back label of the bottle will tell you what to expect: *cosecha* (harvest) means that the wine has not been aged in oak, or alternatively that it's one of the new-wave 'high-expression' wines (the price should indicate which

one); *crianza* means the wine has had at least a year in barrel and a year in bottle before release; *reserva* has had the same plus a further year in barrel or bottle; *gran reserva* has had at least two years in barrel and at least three in bottle.

In today's market, Rioja can be divided into four main types. Of course, every bodega has its own house style and many of them produce a range of wines across all styles, but, broadly speaking, this is what to expect:

Young wines with little or no oak have been made in Rioja since Roman times (the technology has moved on quite a bit since then), and in the Basque Country they are still the most favoured style. Typically made with 100 per cent Tempranillo, the wine is enjoyed young and fresh, sometimes as early as the Christmas after the vintage. In bars and cafés from Laguardia to Bilbao, the bright-purple liquid is drunk with great gusto from flat-bottomed tumblers, and elsewhere in Rioja most bars will have something similar in a house red.

Classic wines are the ones most people recognize as Rioja: full strawberry/raspberry Tempranillo fruit with a background of warm, toasty oak. These are the wines that built Rioja's reputation in the last quarter of the 19th century, and most mainstream houses make examples of them, labelled *crianza*, *reserva* or *gran reserva* according to age. Perhaps the most classic of all Rioja bodegas is López de Heredia in Haro (www.lopezdeheredia.com), which is still making wine in much the same way as it did a century ago and offering 'current' vintages which are 10 and 15 years old.

Modern wines are those which tend to use the minimum oak to maximize the fruit and to allow for earlier drinking. The pioneer of this style was Marqués de Cáceres in Cenicero (www.marquesdecaceres.com), which installed the first all-stainless-steel bodega equipment in Rioja in the 1970s. Modern *crianza* wines often have the bare minimum 12 months in oak and there are also wines that may be labelled *roble*, which might have as few as three or four months in the barrel.

Genericos ('generic wines') started to appear in the late 1990s and don't use the traditional descriptions (*crianza*, etc.). Typically these are very powerful, concentrated wines, and most winemakers claim that what they're trying to do is to get the maximum expression of the terroir into the wine. Two of the pioneers of this style are Roda and Allende (*see* below), and many mainstream bodegas now make a high-expression wine at the top of their range in addition to more traditional styles.

Indeed, given that it's now possible to find wines from the lightest, freshest, early-drinking gluggers to the most modern, blockbusting, high-expression wines, in addition to the ancient classics, there has never been a better time to enjoy Rioja.

OTHER WINES

VdlT Valles de Sadacia

Only in March 2003 were the wines of the Valles de Sadacia classified as VdlT after years of lobbying by the five growers in the vineyards along the banks of the River Cidacos around Calahorra. Only two of these actually make wine and the only example widely available is made under contract by a bodega in Logroño. They grow Moscatel with a little Malvasía and Viura, and the wines may be sweet, dry or anything in between.

Main Bodegas
(listed in alphabetical order), PRODUCER NAME; town/village; web/E-mail address; best wines (r = red, w = white) A star (*) indicates particularly good quality.

DOCa RIOJA
www.riojawine.com
www.winesfromrioja.co.uk

Rioja is a generous wine in quality terms and even the humblest bottle offers a level of reliability unparalleled in most other wine regions. In the selection below, however, constraints of space mean that only a very few of the best and most consistent bodegas can be included: the wines listed are those that have shown the highest quality in recent tastings.

AGRÍCOLA LABASTIDA; Labastida; www.agricolalabastida.com; El Belisario (r)*

ARTADI; Laguardia; www.artadi.com; Viña El Pisón (r)*, Pagos Viejos (r)*

BENJAMÍN ROMEO; San Vicente de la Sonsierra; contador@hotmail.com; Contador (r)*, La Viña de Andrés Romeo (r)*

BERONIA; Ollauri; www.beronia.es; III a.c. (r)*

BILBAÍNAS; Haro; www.bodegasbilbainas.com; La Vicalanda (r)*, Viña Pomal (r)*

BRETÓN; Navarette; www.bodegasbreton.com; Alba de Bretón (r)*, Dominio de Conte (r)*

CONTINO; Laserna-Laguardia; www.contino-sa.com; Graciano (r)*, Viña del Olivo (r)*

CVNE; Haro; www.cvne.com; Real de Asúa (*), Imperial (r)*

FERNÁNDEZ DE MANZANOS; Azagra; www.bodegasfernandezdemanzanos.com; Finca Manzanos Crianza, Reserva (r)*

FINCA ALLENDE; Briones; www.finca-allende.com; Aurus (r)*, Calvario (r)*

GUZMAN ALDAZÁBAL; Navaridas; guzmanaldazabal@terra.es; Exaltación (r)*, Guzmán Aldazábal (r)*

LÓPEZ DE HEREDIA; Haro; www.lopezdeheredia.com; Viña Tondonia Gran Reserva (r, w)*

LUÍS CAÑAS; Villabuena; www.luiscanas.com; Hiru 3 Racimos (r)*, Amaren (r)*

MARQUÉS DE CÁCERES; Cenicero; www.marquesdecaceres.com; Gaudium (r)*, MC (r)*

MARQUÉS DE MURRIETA; Logroño; www.marquesdemurrieta.com; Dalmau (r)*, Reserva (r)*

MIGUEL MERINO; Briones; www.miguelmerino.com; Unnum (r)*, Magnum Gran Reserva (r)*

MUGA; Haro; www.bodegasmuga.es; Selección Especial (r)*, Prado Enea (r)*

OSTATU; Samaniego; www.ostatu.com; Gloria de Ostatu (r)*

PÁGANOS; Páganos-Laguardia; www.eguren.com; El Puntido (r)*, La Nieta (r)*

PALACIO; Laguardia; www.bodegaspalacio.es; Reserva Especial (r)*

PALACIOS REMONDO; Alfaro; www.palacioremondo.com; Plácet (w)*, Propriedad (r)*

PUJANZA; Laguardia; www.bodegaspujanza.com; Pujanza (r)*, Pujanza Norte (r)*

RAMÓN BILBAO; Haro; www.bodegasramonbilbao.es; Mirto (r)*

REMELLURI; Labastida; www.remelluri.com; Colección Jaime Rodríguez (r)*, Reserva (r)*

REMÍREZ DE GANUZA; Samaniego; www.remirezdeganuza.com; Trasnocho (r)*, Reserva (r)*

RIOJANAS; Cenicero; www.bodegasriojanas.com; Gran Albina (r)*, Gran Albina Vendimia (r)*

RODA; Haro; www.roda.es; Cirsión (r)*, Roda I (r)*

SEÑORÍO DE SAN VICENTE; San Vicente de la Sonsierra; www.eguren.com; San Vicente (r)*

SIERRA CANTABRIA; San Vicente de la Sonsierra; www.eguren.com; Organza (w)*, El Bosque (r)*

TOBÍA; San Asensio; www.bodegastobia.com; Alma de Tobia (r)*, Óscar Tobía (r)*

VALDEMAR; Oyón; www.martinezbujanda.com; Inspiración Valdemar Graciano (r)*

VALSACRO; Pradejón; www.valsacro.com; Dioro (r)*, Valsacro (r)*

VdlT VALLES DE SADACIA

ONTAÑÓN; Logroño; www.ontanon.es; Marco Fabio (w)

Madrid is a thriving European capital of spacious boulevards and heroic fountains, large corporations and long lunches. The teeming streets of the old town, dominated by the Plaza Mayor, are surrounded by architectural developments that date back to the early 19th-century and give Madrid its cosmopolitan atmosphere. Yet Madrid is more than just a city: it's a province and an autonomous community with its own parliament.

From a food point of view, tapas are probably Madrid's staple diet; the bars around the Plaza Santa Ana are a particular magnet for lunchtime and early evening crowds before they hit the restaurants at about 9pm – where you can eat the food of every region of Spain, and most other

Madrid

countries, in the city. There are, however, some traditional dishes that survive here. One of the most famous is the *cocido madrileño*: a nourishing mix of vegetables and meat – indeed, anything poor families could find – which can be a hefty soup or a substantial stew.

LOCAL SPECIALITIES

Madrid has, however, not forgotten its gastronomic roots. Outside the city the countryside is rural, and known for its farms and smallholders.

A favourite is beef from the Sierra de Guadarrama north and west of the city, where they farm Avileña-Negra Ibérica, Limusina and Charolais cattle.

Aceitunas de Campo Real are table olives (as opposed to olives for making oil) from Campo Real, which is about 35km (22 miles) east of the city. In terms of olive oil, *aceite de oliva virgen de Madrid* comes from olive groves in the southern part of the province.

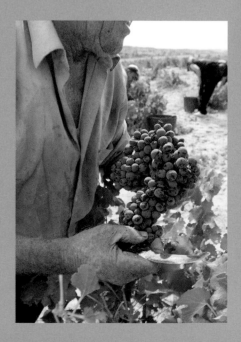

Vegetables and fruit are legion, including *ajo blanco de Chinchón* ('white' garlic), *espárragos de Aranjuez* (asparagus) and *garbanzos y lentejas de Madrid* (beans and lentils). And there's a general classification, *hortalizas de Madrid*, for other vegetables seen as particularly good. *Melones de Villaconejos* (melons from Villaconejos), are grown 50km (31 miles) south of the city.

Dairy products include *queso de cabra de Madrid* (goat's cheese) and *queso puro de oveja de Madrid* (sheep's cheese), both from accredited farms. There's also a classified *leche pasteurizado de Madrid* for milk from accredited herds, as well as a category for *huevos de Madrid* (eggs).

Roasted suckling pig is one of the star dishes in the region of Madrid. In my family's restaurant, it's the only dish that, when properly cooked, reminds me that I belong to the third generation of chefs in the family. Each season, the flavour seems to change slightly, but the roasting technique remains the same. Cooking the pork in this way guarantees that the meat is not greasy and the crackling is very crunchy.

Cochinillo lacado sobre turrón de patata y almendra con tomillo limonero

Glazed suckling pig served on potato and almond nougat with lemon thyme

INGREDIENTS (SERVES 4)

1 piglet
100ml (3¹/2fl oz) olive oil
salt, to taste
1 heaped tablespoon ground
   black pepper
100ml (3¹/2fl oz) vinegar

FOR POTATO AND ALMOND NOUGAT

500g (1lb 2oz) potatoes, peeled
   and chopped
1 onion, chopped
extra-virgin olive oil
100g (3¹/2oz), blanched almonds,
   roughly chopped
250ml (9fl oz) milk
1 teaspoon agar agar
salt and pepper to taste
sprigs of fresh lemon thyme,
   to garnish

Make the potato and almond nougat the day before roasting the piglet. Preheat the oven to 60°C (140°F). Put the potatoes and onion in a roasting tin, cover with olive oil and cook in the oven for 1 hour. Remove the potatoes and onions from the olive oil and drain in a colander.

Toast the almonds under the grill until golden. Pour the milk into a flameproof casserole, add the almonds and potatoes and bring to the boil over a high heat. Turn down the heat and simmer until the potatoes start to break up. Stir in the agar agar, season with salt and pepper and beat well. Pack the potato-almond mash into a shallow rectangular dish. Set aside to cool, before putting in the refrigerator for 24 hours.

The next day, preheat the oven to 200°C (400°F, gas mark 6). Season the skin of the piglet with olive oil and salt, and inside the body cavity with salt, pepper, olive oil and vinegar. Lay the piglet on its back in a heavy-based roasting tin and roast for 1 hour. Then turn the piglet over, taking care not to splash the hot fat, so its back faces upward. Roast for another hour until the skin is dark golden brown and the crackling crunchy. All the fat should drain to the bottom of the roasting tin.

When the piglet is cooked through, remove from the oven and leave to rest for 10 minutes before serving. Turn the potato and almond nougat out of the dish onto a chopping board and cut into slices.

Place a slice of the potato and almond nougat on each plate and put a piece of suckling pig on top. Garnish with sprigs of fresh lemon thyme.

WINE TIPS

SPECIAL OCCASION: **El Rincón, Marqués de Griñón (€€€)**
SUNDAY LUNCH: **Montazo, Telmo Rodríguez (€€)**
EVERYDAY: **Maín Reserva, Orusco (€)**

Cooked properly, the *tortilla de patatas* (classic Spanish omelette) can be brilliant. In spite of its simple ingredients – eggs, potatoes, onions and olive oil – it's an iconic dish, served in all the bars and restaurants in the region and city of Madrid. A good *tortilla* has to be moist, but never greasy. This exciting recipe pushes the boundaries of a homely dish to new horizons of taste, texture and sophistication.

Tortilla en los pasos de la evolución
Evolutionary Spanish omelette

INGREDIENTS (SERVES 4)

FOR THE HOT POTATO FROTH
500g (1lb 2oz) potatoes, peeled
   and chopped
olive oil
250ml (9fl oz) double cream
pinch of salt
1 sifón iSi

FOR THE CARAMELIZED ONIONS
250g (9oz) onions, peeled, halved
   and finely sliced
100g (3½oz) caster sugar
olive oil

FOR THE SABAYON
3 egg yolks
pinch of salt
2 sheets of leaf gelatine, soaked
   in cold water
1 sifón iSi

GARNISH
sea salt
fresh parsley, finely chopped

For the hot potato froth, preheat the oven to 75°C (165°F). Put the potatoes in a roasting tin, cover with olive oil and cook in the oven for 2 hours.

To caramelize the onions, spread out the raw onions in a roasting tin and sprinkle over the sugar. Drench in olive oil and cook gently in the same oven as the potatoes for at least 2 hours. Stir the onions frequently. (The success of the dish depends on turning the onions regularly.)

When the potatoes are cooked, drain off the olive oil and put the potato pieces in a food processor. Pour the cream into a saucepan and warm over a gentle heat, then pour over the potatoes in the food processor. Add the salt and blend thoroughly to form a smooth, runny purée. Pour into a cream-whipping siphon fitted with a nitrous oxide gas cylinder and stand in a bain-marie to keep warm.

To make the sabayon (frothy egg whip), put the egg yolks in a bowl with a pinch of salt and beat with a whisk. Add 1 tablespoon of hot water and whisk until the yolks have tripled in volume. Add the gelatine and pour the mixture into another cream-whipping siphon fitted with a nitrous oxide gas cylinder. Stand the siphon in the top of a double-saucepan over simmering water to maintain a constant temperature.

Serve in heatproof cocktail glasses: a pina colada glass is the right shape to contain the two frothy elements. Put a teaspoon of the caramelized onions into each glass. Shake the sabayon siphon well, then squirt a burst of frothy sabayon over the onions. Then shake the potato siphon and crown with a squirt of hot potato froth. Garnish with a pinch of sea salt and a sprinkling of fresh parsley.

WINE TIPS
SPECIAL OCCASION: 750, Nueva Valverde (€€€)
SUNDAY LUNCH: Asido, Ricardo Benito (€€)
EVERYDAY: Puerta del Sol Varietales, Jeromín (€)

This substantial dish appears in almost every old Madrid recipe book. Its origins can be traced back to the *olla podrida* (hotpot) from La Mancha. Traditionally, the stew is simmered for a long time over a low heat in an earthenware pot, although these days, when time is short, most people usually cook it in a pressure cooker.

Cocido Madrileño
Chickpea stew with vegetables and assorted meats

INGREDIENTS (SERVES 4)

400g (14oz) dried chickpeas
600g (1lb 5oz) veal shank
1 piece of pig's knuckle
2 veal bones, with bone marrow
100g (3½oz) salt pork
1 breast and 1 leg of chicken
1 onion, peeled and studded with
    2 cloves
6 carrots, peeled
4 potatoes, peeled
½ cabbage, coarsely shredded
300g (10½oz) fine green beans
2 *chorizos*, 20cm (8in) long
2 *morcillas de cebolla*, or black
    pudding, 20cm (8in) long

FOR THE DUMPLINGS

2 slices of bread, finely crumbed
1 egg
1 tablespoon chopped fresh
    parsley
1 garlic clove, crushed
meat stock
olive oil, for deep frying
1 garlic clove, crushed
lots of olive oil
pinch of salt

Put the chickpeas in a large bowl, cover with cold water and soak overnight.

Rinse the veal, pig's knuckle, veal bones and salt pork under cold running water. Trim any fat from the chicken. Place all the meat (except the chicken) in a large flameproof casserole, cover with water and bring to the boil over a high heat. From time to time, skim off any residue that rises to the surface.

When the water is boiling, tip in the onion and chickpeas and boil steadily for 1 hour. Then add the chicken, carrots and potatoes, turn down the heat to low and simmer gently for another hour, or until the meats are cooked through.

To make the dumplings, mix the breadcrumbs, egg, parsley and garlic together in a bowl and add enough meat stock to make a stiff paste. Shape the paste into small balls, then fry in a frying pan with plenty of olive oil, until golden all over. When the meat mixture has cooked for at least 2 hours, drop the dumplings into the casserole and simmer for another 30 minutes. Then drain off the stock into a separate saucepan, add a pinch of salt and serve as a soup.

Bring a saucepan of lightly salted cold water to the boil and drop in the cabbage and green beans. Boil for 15 minutes, then drain and set aside. Place the *chorizos* and *morcillas* in another saucepan with some hot meat stock from the casserole and simmer for 30 minutes until heated through. Cut into smaller pieces and set aside.

This dish is usually served in three *vuelcos* (turns): as a soup, followed by servings of chickpeas, potatoes, cabbage and green beans, and then the meat and sausages, with the dumplings alongside.

WINE TIPS

SPECIAL OCCASION: **Qubél Reserva, Gosálbez Orti (€€€)**
SUNDAY LUNCH: **Tagonius Crianza (€€)**
EVERYDAY: **Jesús Diaz Tinto (€)**

Migas, which literally translates as 'breadcrumbs', was originally a humble shepherds' dish, but from such tiny crumbs, some sensational desserts have been devised. In this particular sweet flight of fancy, *migas* is transformed into a trend-setting dessert, with a chocolate-flavoured nutty crumble providing a crunchy contrast to creamy frozen yogurt and frothy white chocolate.

Migas de chocolate del siglo XXI

Twenty-first century chocolate 'breadcrumbs'

INGREDIENTS (SERVES 4)

FOR THE FROZEN YOGURT
100ml (3¹/₂fl oz) milk
200ml (7fl oz) double cream
125g (4¹/₂oz) caster sugar
100g (3¹/₂oz) Greek yogurt
4 tablespoons powdered yogurt

FOR THE *MIGAS*
200g (7oz) butter, softened
200g (7oz) plain flour
3 tablespoons cocoa powder
200g (7oz) soft light brown sugar
200g (7oz) assorted blanched
    almonds and hazelnuts

FOR THE WHITE CHOCOLATE FROTH
250ml (9fl oz) milk
150ml (5fl oz) double cream
250ml (9fl oz) condensed milk
350g (12oz) white chocolate
    couverture (cooking chocolate)
3 sheets of leaf gelatine, soaked
    in cold water
1 sifón iSi

To make the frozen yogurt, put the milk, cream and sugar in a saucepan and bring slowly to the boil over a medium heat, stirring constantly. Remove from the heat and leave to cool. Then stir in the fresh and powdered yogurts, pour into a plastic container and put in the freezer to set overnight.

To make the *migas*, preheat the oven to 190°C (375°F, gas mark 5). Put the butter, flour, cocoa, sugar and nuts in a food processor and blend for two 45-second bursts, or until the nuts are finely chopped. Then spread the crumble mixture onto a baking tray with a spatula. Bake in the oven for 20 minutes. Remove from the oven and leave to cool slightly. While still warm, break up into fine crumbs with a fork.

For the white chocolate froth, pour the milk, cream and condensed milk into a saucepan and bring to the boil. Take off the heat, add the white chocolate and stir until melted. Then stir in the gelatine until it has dissolved. When cool, pour the chocolate cream into a cream-whipping siphon fitted with a nitrous oxide gas cylinder and chill in the refrigerator. Shake the siphon well before piping the chocolate froth.

Pipe some white chocolate froth on one side of each bowl. In the centre, pile up a heap of chocolate *migas* and place a scoop of frozen yogurt beside the crumbs.

WINE TIPS

SPECIAL OCCASION: **Moscatel Chivite 125** (€€€)
SUNDAY LUNCH: **Olivares Dulce Monastrell** (€€)
EVERYDAY: **Blanco Semidulce Alma de Valdeguerra** (€)

Madrid wines and bodegas

The winemaking tradition in the Madrid area goes back to the 13th century, but the region wasn't promoted to full DO status until 1990 under the name *Vinos de Madrid* to avoid confusion with the *autonomía*, province and city. This is the only DO zone in the province. On the face of it you'd expect a wine-producing area within the community of one of the world's largest capital cities to be fully geared up in terms of supplying its local market, but this has not been the case, partly because of the dominance of Rioja (as is the case all over Spain), partly, perhaps, because a prophet is always without honour in his own country, but mainly because, as recently as the mid-1990s, the wines were, quite simply, of no interest to anyone outside the village in which they had been made: perilously high in alcohol, boiled to death during fermentation and often oxidized before they went into the bottle. Meanwhile, regions further afield, such as La Mancha and Valdepeñas, had leapfrogged the Madrid winelands to take the capital's café-bar market, while the city's best restaurants stuck to fine-wine areas such as Rioja and Ribera del Duero.

The regulations were changed in the late 1990s to allow for a more modern style and work began on trying to persuade *Madrileños* to try the wines from their own community. After years of prejudice, that work is still going on, but there's no doubt that Madrid is now producing at least some world-class wines.

The vineyards of Madrid offer a range of qualities: here, there are wines that don't hit the high notes of the quality scale. There are also some excellent wines that are being vigorously marketed by the companies that make them, and are proud of them; a special mention must be made for Ricardo Benito, whose Divo is unquestionably one of the finest wines of Spain.

The DO's proximity to the city of Madrid, with its burgeoning market and ever-increasing prosperity, should provide all the stimulus necessary to get the best out of its growers and winemakers in the long term. The vineyards are high enough to avoid the worst of summer heat (Madrid city is the highest capital in Europe at 646m/2,100ft), which provides an advantage in the ripening season (hot days and cold nights), and some stars are beginning to emerge among the DO's bodegas.

The vineyard area is split into three subzones in a kind of semicircle around the south of the city of Madrid, all named after the chief towns within them. Arganda is to the southeast, Navalcarnero to the west and south, and San Martín de Valdeiglesias to the west. The bodegas make all kinds of wine – red, pink, white and sparkling – and also a local traditional wine in Arganda called *sobremadre* (literally 'over mother'), which is fermented on its lees (the squashed grape skins and, indeed, 'mother' of the wine) and left to mature in the tank for six months prior to bottling. It's hefty stuff.

For white, sweet and sparkling wines, they grow the Malvar, Airén, Albillo, Viura, Parellada, Torrontés and Moscatel grapes. For reds, there's Tempranillo (here known also as *Tinto Fino* and *Tinto de Madrid*), Garnacha, Merlot, Cabernet Sauvignon, Syrah and Monastrell. The best wines are probably the reds made with Tempranillo, usually with a minority inclusion of Cabernet, Merlot, Syrah and/or others. However, some interesting and good-value whites are made from the Malvar and barrel-fermented. This is an emerging region with great promise for the future, if star wines are a little few and far between at the moment.

OTHER DRINKS

The province of Madrid is also famous throughout Spain for an anise liqueur distilled in the town of Chinchón, about 40km (25 miles) south-west of the city. Both anise and grapes are grown locally; grape growers send their surplus wine for distillation and green anise seeds are marinated in the spirit before it is redistilled in copper pot-stills. The spirit is made in several styles from dry (the strongest at over 70 per cent abv; sometimes known colloquially as 'brain-damage in a bottle') to sweet, with added sugar and at a lower strength. It's normally drunk as a *digestivo* after a meal, with water, ice or even in coffee. It is rumoured to have medicinal qualities and is popular with ladies 'of a certain age' to alleviate arthritis. There is only one distillery remaining in Chinchón and it now belongs to the Sherry giant González Byass (www.gonzalezbyass.com).

Main Bodegas
(listed in alphabetical order), PRODUCER NAME; town/village; web/E-mail address; best wines (r = red, w = white) A star (*) indicates particularly good quality.

Details of all bodegas are available at www.vinosdemadrid.es

GOSÁLBEZ ORTI; Pozuelo del Rey (Arganda); www.qubel.com; Qubél (r)*

JEROMÍN; Villarejo de Salvanés (Arganda); www.vinosjeromin.com; Puerta del Sol (w), Félix Martín, Grego, Manu (r)*

NUEVA VALVERDE; Villa del Prado (San Martín de Valdeiglesias); www.bodegasnuevavalverde.com; Tejoneras (r), 750 (r)*

RICARDO BENITO; Navalcarnero; www.ricardobenito.com; Divo (r)*, Tapon de Oro

TAGONIUS; Tielmes (Arganda); tagonius@reova.com; Tagonius (r)

Geographically, Murcia is part of the Levant, yet when the new regional Spain was created after the return to democracy, it became one of the seven single-province *autonomías*, independent of Valencia to the east and Castilla-La Mancha (New Castile) and Andalucía to the west. The reasons for this go back a long way. When the Moors were finally expelled from Spain in 1492, much of the land south of Madrid was scorched as a result of the battles between the Castilian and Moorish forces, and the crown offered land concessions to anyone prepared to move to this former war zone and cultivate it. Many people who had fled the war came back and restarted their farming lives, but they were Castilians and spoke Castellano. Over the border in Valencia they spoke (and still

Murcia

speak) Valençà, a dialect of Catalan, and this explains the difference: Levantine geography, Castilian culture and language.

This agricultural renascence has given the region a rich culture of farming, which prevails to the present day. Murcia is the largest of the single-province *autonomías* and a great deal of its land is given over to food and wine production.

LOCAL SPECIALITIES

Meat products include the inevitable *jamón serrano* and *cordero* (lamb) *Segureña* (a local breed), plus cheese. *Queso de Murcia* is made from the milk of the local Murciano-Granadino goat, semi-hard and often flavoured with rosemary and tarragon, and it comes *fresco* (fresh), *curado* ('cured' – i.e. aged) and *al vino* (marinated in wine), and there's also a *queso de cabra curado á la almendra* (goat's cheese cured with almonds).

Murcia is a positive cornucopia of fresh produce: almost anything will grow in this fertile area. There is rice from Calasparra, about 70km (44 miles) north-west of Murcia city, pears from Jumilla (better known for its wine; *see* page 159) and region-wide production of *pimentón de Murcia*, red peppers of the Bola variety, dried and rendered into powder for cooking. Other produce grown across the region includes almonds, celery, broccoli, cauliflower, cabbage, endive (frisée), lettuce, olives and tomatoes. Fruits include citrus fruit, table grapes, melons, watermelons and *frutales de hueso*: stone fruits such as plums, peaches, etc. In addition, of course, as with almost every other region of Spain, olive oil is a major product.

In the heartland of Murcia, vegetables reign supreme in dishes where freshness and eye-catching colour are important. *Zarangollo* (an omelette) is a typical example of the Murcian approach to food. This avant-garde take on the *Zarangollo* is made without eggs and with the addition of fresh cod, which gives the dish an extremely stylish appearance and taste.

Zarangollo Murciano

Deconstructed tomato, potato and vegetable 'omelette' with cod and beetroot

INGREDIENTS (SERVES 4)

250ml (9fl oz) olive oil

2 onions, finely chopped

1 red pepper, finely chopped

3 tomatoes

500g (1lb 2oz) pumpkin, chopped

500g (1lb 2oz) potatoes, half roughly chopped, half cut into 3cm- (1¼in-) thick slices

3 bay leaves

10g (¼oz) agar agar

30g (1oz) fresh dill

200g (7oz) cod fillet

100g (3½oz) cooked beetroot

8 deep-fried basil leaves

100g (3½oz) black tapioca pearls

FOR THE BISCAY SAUCE

4 garlic cloves, finely chopped

1 onion, finely chopped

200g (7oz) bread, cut into cubes

3 *choricero* peppers

100g (3½oz) plain flour

250ml (9fl oz) chicken stock

salt and pepper to taste

Heat 1 tablespoon of the olive oil in a frying pan over a medium heat. Add the onions and pepper, sauté until softened but not browned, then set aside in a bowl. Skin, deseed and chop the tomatoes. Pour another 2 tablespoons of the olive oil into the frying pan and sauté the pumpkin, chopped potatoes, bay leaves and tomatoes until cooked. Remove the bay leaves and put the vegetables and tomatoes into a food processor, add the agar agar and blend to a smooth purée.

Preheat the oven to 170°C (325°F, gas mark 3). Put the sliced potatoes in an ovenproof dish with the dill and 3 tablespoons of the olive oil and bake in the oven for 40 minutes until soft. Set aside. Put the cod in a separate ovenproof dish with 3 tablespoons of the olive oil and bake in the same oven for 15 minutes until just cooked. Leave to cool before flaking the cod, then set aside.

Thinly slice the cooked beetroot. Heat the remaining olive oil in a frying pan over a medium heat. Fry the slices of beetroot until crunchy. In the same oil, fry the basil leaves until crisp. Set both aside. Soften the tapioca in boiling water.

To make the Biscay sauce, heat 3 tablespoons of olive oil in a frying pan over a medium heat. Add the garlic, onion, bread and *choricero* peppers and sauté until golden. Mix in the flour with a wooden spoon, then add the stock and stir until the sauce thickens. Season with salt and pepper. Press through a sieve, leaving a sauce with a thick texture.

In the base of a dish, place 3 drops of the Biscay sauce and on top of each, place some thick-sliced potato and then a portion of purée. On top of each portion, place a few slices of cod and garnish with black tapioca pearls, beetroot and deep-fried basil.

WINE TIPS

SPECIAL OCCASION: **Clio, El Nido, Jumilla (€€€)**

SUNDAY LUNCH: **Partal Selección 37 Barricas, Balcona, Bullas (€€)**

EVERYDAY: **Castaño Monastrell, Yecla (€)**

With 170km (106 miles) of coastline, it is hardly surprising that much of Murcia's food comes from the sea. Fish such as horse mackerel, whitebait and Atlantic mackerel often appear on the menu. Here, a popular delicacy, *pargo* (porgy or sea bream) is served with peaches, which have been grown in the region since Roman times.

Lomo de pargo asado con esencia de crustáceos y melocotón confitado

Grilled sea bream with shellfish essence and peach confit

INGREDIENTS (SERVES 4)

2kg (4lb 8oz) sea bream, filleted

5 tomatoes

2 onions, sliced

30g (1oz) pine kernels

4 garlic cloves, sliced

1 tablespoon chopped parsley

salt and pepper, to taste

100ml (3½fl oz) olive oil

500ml (18fl oz) white wine

200g (7oz) green *piquillo* peppers

2 teaspoons dried oregano

2 teaspoons dried thyme

200g (7oz) each small crabs and
    spider crabs, shelled, shells saved

400g (14oz) prawns, shelled,
    shells saved

400g (14oz) raw king prawns,
    shelled, shells saved

100g (3 1/2oz) caster sugar

200g (7oz) peaches, sliced

1 teaspoon balsamic vinegar

1 teaspoon fresh thyme

1 teaspoon fresh rosemary

Preheat the oven to 180°C (350°F, gas mark 4). Cut the fish fillets into 175g (6oz) pieces and place skin-side down in a roasting tin. Slice 1 tomato and arrange the slices around the fish along with the onion slices. Scatter the pine kernels on top with half the garlic. Sprinkle with chopped parsley, salt and pepper. Drizzle with 2 tablespoons olive oil and pour the wine on top along with 1 litre (1¼ pint) water. Put the roasting tin in an oven for about 15 minutes until the fish is cooked.

Meanwhile, put the *piquillo* peppers on a baking tray and roast in the oven for 12 minutes. Then tip into a food processor and blend to a purée. Strain the purée to remove skin, seeds and stalk. Remove the soft flesh from the remaining tomatoes, purée them, add to the pepper purée and season with the oregano and thyme.

Put the shells of the crabs and prawns into a saucepan and barely cover with water. Bring to the boil, then simmer on a low heat for 20 minutes to make a stock. Strain through a sieve into a clean saucepan and reduce over a low heat to make a sauce.

In small saucepan, stir the caster sugar and 50ml (2fl oz) cold water together over a high heat until the sugar has dissolved (about 6 minutes). Add the peaches and cook for a further 2 minutes until you have a golden, caramelized syrup. Set aside.

Heat 2 tablespoons of oil in a frying pan and fry the remaining garlic until crunchy. Brush the prawns with oil and grill for 4 minutes, turning once, until pink all over.

Draw a few lines with the pepper purée in the middle of a plate. Place a piece of fish in the centre, arrange 5 peach slices around it and place the prawns and crab on top. Bathe in reduced fish stock. Garnish with a drizzle of balsamic vinegar and olive oil, the crunchy garlic and fresh rosemary and thyme.

WINE TIPS

SPECIAL OCCASION: **Manuel Manzaneque Chardonnay, Finca Élez (DO Pago, Castilla-La Mancha) (€€€)**

SUNDAY LUNCH: **Casa de la Ermita Viognier, Jumilla (€€)**

EVERYDAY: **Valcorso fermentado en barrica, La Purísima, Yecla (€)**

Better known as a tourist destination for watersports enthusiasts, the maritime lagoon of the Mar Menor is also one of the finest fishing areas for catching king prawns and grey mussels. Regional seafood plays a leading role in this recipe, together with the rice of Calasparra, whose short, plump grains are capable of absorbing intense flavours.

Arroz meloso de Calasparra con langostino del Mar Menor y queso al aroma de vino tinto

Sweet Calasparra rice with king prawns and wine-scented cheese

INGREDIENTS (SERVES 4)

300g (10¹/₂oz) fish bones
500ml (18fl oz) water
2 garlic cloves
100g (3¹/₂oz) fresh parsley, chopped
2 tablespoons olive oil
2 onions, chopped
1 tablespoon plain flour
250ml (9fl oz) white wine
125ml (4fl oz) squid ink
salt and pepper to taste
a few sprigs of fresh parsley
250ml (9fl oz) olive oil
250ml (9fl oz) red wine
325g (11¹/₂oz) *calasparra* rice
500ml (18fl oz) hot beef stock
55g (2oz) cream cheese
1 tablespoon raisins, marinated in
    sweet red wine
1 tablespoon pine kernels
400g (14oz) raw king prawns,
    peeled

To make a fish stock, put the fish bones and water in a large saucepan. Bring to the boil over a high heat, then simmer over a low heat for 30 minutes. Strain the stock through a sieve into a clean saucepan over a very low heat to keep warm. Grind the garlic and parsley to a paste in a pestle and mortar.

Heat the olive oil in a large saucepan over a medium heat and sauté the onions. Mix the flour into the frying pan with a wooden spoon and cook for 1 minute. Add the white wine, stirring continuously as the sauce thickens. Gradually stir in half the ground garlic and parsley, and enough fish stock to thin the sauce. When the sauce begins to boil, add the squid ink, salt and pepper. Turn down the heat to low and simmer gently until the sauce thickens; set aside.

Blend the parsley sprigs and olive oil in a food processor for 1 minute to make an oil.

Bring the red wine to a boil in a pan, reduce the heat and simmer until thickened.

Heat 4 tablespoons of olive oil in a saucepan and sauté the remaining garlic and parsley. Stir in the rice, then gradually add the beef stock: add 175ml (6fl oz) at a time, stirring continuously, and wait until the stock has been absorbed by the rice before adding more. When all the beef stock has been added, use some of the remaining hot fish stock to keep the rice moist until cooked. Then stir in the cream cheese, raisins, pine kernels, salt and pepper.

Brush the king prawns with olive oil, grill for 4 minutes, turning, until pink all over.

Spoon a trail of squid ink base across each plate. Spoon some the rice on top and crown with the king prawns. Drizzle some parsley oil and red wine reduction around the plates.

WINE TIPS

SPECIAL OCCASION: **Viña Tondonia Rosado Crianza, López de Heredia (€€€)**
SUNDAY LUNCH: **Alceño Rosado, Pedro Luís Martínez, Jumilla (€€)**
EVERYDAY: **Castillo de Jumilla Monastrell Rosado, Bleda, Jumilla (€)**

Paparajotes are always served on St George's Day, which is celebrated on 19 March in Spain. This unusual Murcian dessert is made with lemon leaves. Although the leaves are never eaten, they form a platform on which to fry the batter and infuse it with a sublime lemon flavour. This dessert is typical of the *barracas* (urban open-air cafés), which suddenly pop up in Murcia with the arrival of spring.

Paparajotes

Lemon leaves deep-fried with eggs and cinnamon

INGREDIENTS (SERVES 4)

1 litre (1³/4 pint) milk

700ml (1¹/4 pint) water

6 eggs, separated

500g (1lb 2oz) self-raising flour

juice of 1 lemon

ground cinnamon, to taste

650g (1lb 7oz) caster sugar

500ml (18fl oz) vegetable oil

24 lemon leaves, washed

2 tablespoons icing sugar and
    1 teaspoon cinnamon, sifted
    together, for dusting the leaves
    and for the sweet spicy millk

200g (7oz) Emmental cheese, diced

2 tablespoons plain flour

1 egg, well beaten

100g (3¹/2oz) blueberry jam

2 tablespoons agar agar

4 sheets of leaf gelatine, soaked

1 sifón iSi

200g (7oz) fresh redcurrants

30g (1oz) fresh mint, to garnish

Beat together 850ml (1½ pint) milk, the water and egg yolks in a bowl. Sprinkle in the flour gradually, beating to stop lumps forming. Beat in the lemon juice, cinnamon and 400g (14oz) of the caster sugar. Whisk the egg whites into stiff peaks and fold into the batter. Heat the oil in a saucepan. Dip the lemon leaves in the batter and fry in batches until crisp and golden. Drain on kitchen paper. Dust with icing sugar and cinnamon.

Toss the Emmental cheese in flour, then dip in egg and fry for a few seconds in very hot oil. Drain on kitchen paper and set aside.

To make a syrup, put the remaining sugar and 3 tablespoons of water in a saucepan. Heat, over a medium heat, stirring until the sugar dissolves, then leave to simmer until fine strands form. Stir in the jam and agar agar until dissolved. Pour the mixture into a small rectangular dish and chill until set – it should be translucent and soft but firm.

Put the remaining milk, cinnamon and icing sugar into a *thermomix* (food processor that cooks). Blend at speed 6 and at 100°C (210°F) for 5 minutes. Add the gelatine and blend for 3 more minutes. Pour the sweet spicy milk into a cream-whipping siphon fitted with a nitrous oxide gas cylinder and set aside to cool for 2 hours.

Make a caramel to glaze the redcurrants. In small saucepan, stir 100g (3½oz) caster sugar and 100ml (3½fl oz) cold water together over a high heat until the sugar has dissolved. Continue to heat until the syrup is golden. Remove from the heat immediately and carefully dip the bunches of redcurrants into the caramel.

Put a slice of the blueberry jelly and a few Emmental cubes on each plate. Arrange 6 crisp battered lemon leaves on top. Finish with a cloud of cinnamon froth and the caramelized redcurrants. Garnish with a few sprigs of fresh mint.

WINE TIPS

SPECIAL OCCASION: **Castaño Monastrell Dulce, Yecla (€€€)**

SUNDAY LUNCH: **Dulce María Jesús de Castilla Luzón, Jumilla (€€)**

EVERYDAY: **Casa de la Ermita Dulce, Jumilla (€)**

Wines of Murcia

Murcia is something of a newcomer to wine production at an international level. Although the Jumilla DO was created in 1966, it didn't produce anything of note until the mid-1990s. The same applies to Yecla (1975), whose rise to fame is thanks largely to the efforts of one bodega (Castaño), which drove quality forwards at a time when few importers were interested in emergent regions. The most recent addition is Bullas (1994) and it has jumped on the quality bandwagon created by its two neighbours.

The main grape is the Monastrell (aka Mourvèdre), which was always used to make high-strength wines to be sold to other regions (and other countries) to beef up thin reds. In the early 1990s, somebody dared to try something original with the grape and it proved to have hidden depths: richness, power, even a bit of elegance when treated with respect. Since then, Tempranillo and Garnacha have increased in area, and Cabernet Sauvignon, Merlot and Syrah have been introduced, with sometimes blockbusting effect. There are also white wines made from Airén, Macabeo and Pedro Ximénez, but in this hot, southern climate the reds tend to dominate.

DO BULLAS

A large area, occupying most of the western half of Murcia. The vineyards can be high: from 400m to 800m (1,312–2,625ft). Main grapes are the Monastrell and Tempranillo, and wines are mainly red.

DO JUMILLA

Around the town of the same name, this was the flame that lit the beacon for Murcia in about 1994, with the news that the Monastrell grape really could compete.

DO YECLA

The only DO in Spain relating to a single town, this is another whose best wines also tend to be made from Monastrell.

OTHER WINES

There are two country-wine areas in Murcia. VdlT Campo de Cartagena on the south-east coast makes sweet wines from Tempranillo and Monastrell. VdlT Abanilla, adjacent to the Alicante DO, makes red and white wines of everyday quality.

Main Bodegas

(listed in alphabetical order), PRODUCER NAME; town/village; web/E-mail address; best wines (r = red, w = white) A star (*) indicates particularly good quality.

DO BULLAS
www.bullas.es/vino

BALCONA; Cehegín; www.partal-vinos.com; Partal (r)

DO JUMILLA
www.crdo-jumilla.com

AGAPITO RICO; Jumilla; www.carchelo.com; Carchelo (r)*

BLEDA; Jumilla; www.bodegasbleda.com; Castillo de Jumilla (r)

CASA DE LA ERMITA; Jumilla; www.casadelaermita.com; Monasterio de Santa Ana (r)*, Casa de la Ermita Reserva (r)*

EL NIDO; Jumilla; www.bodegaselnido.com; El Nido (r)*, Clio (r)*

JULIA ROCH E HIJOS; Jumilla; www.casacastillo.es; Casa Castillo Pie Franco (r)*

LUZÓN; Jumilla; www.bodegasluzon.com; Altos de Luzón (r)*, Castillo de Luzón (r)

DO YECLA
www.yeclavino.com

CASTAÑO; Yecla; www.bodegascastano.com; Viña al Lado de la Casa (r)*, Monastrell Dulce (sweet r)*

LA PURÍSIMA; Yecla; www.calpyecla.com; Trapio (r), Iglesia Vieja (r)

A thousand years ago, the Kingdom of Navarre covered most of northern Spain between Galicia and Barcelona as well as a sizeable slice of south-western France. Over the next several centuries it changed hands a number of times. Indeed, Louis XVI of France styled himself 'King of France and Navarre' until 1792. In the meantime, the original kingdom had shrunk to become the region we know today as Navarra, and, in return for a royal charter, it agreed to become part of Spain in 1512. Today, it's a single-province, self-governing region, and one of the most prosperous in Spain. Part of its early prosperity was thanks to the Camino de Santiago, the first 'tourist route' in Europe, which brought pilgrims and churchmen from all over the Continent

Navarra

heading for Santiago de Compostela. Shakespeare set his play *Love's Labours Lost* in what was then Navarre, and the opening speech declares 'Navarre shall be the wonder of the world!'.

LOCAL SPECIALITIES

Navarra has always been one of the *huertas* (market gardens) of Spain: a richly fertile landscape where anything from asparagus to olive trees will thrive. *Esparragós de Navarra* (a *denominación* shared with neighbouring Aragón), the famous white asparagus that is grown underground, is eaten fresh from March to June but usually bottled or tinned for consumption all the year round. *Alcachofa de Tudela* is a special variety of globe artichoke grown in 32 towns and villages

around Tudela, in the deep south of the region, harvested sometimes as early as February. *Pimiento del piquillo de Lodosa* comes from eight villages around Lodosa, near the border with La Rioja. The peppers are a species unique to Navarra and are eaten fresh and roasted as well as being bottled and tinned.

Navarra is livestock-farming country, too, and *ternera de Navarra* is beef taken from the native Pirenaica cattle, believed to have originated in northern Navarra. *Cordero de Navarra* is lamb from anywhere in the region, from the Navarra and Lacha/Latxa (mainly in the north) breeds. These same sheep provide milk for the cheese from Roncal; they graze the high pastures of the Pyrenees and the cheese is made from December to July: firm without being hard, with a strong, spicy flavour.

Navarra is also renowned for its dairy products: Idiazábal is probably the region's most famous cheese. It's made from the unpasteurized milk of Latxa and Carranzana sheep, grazed in the Pyrenees. When mature, the cheese is crumbly, with a sharp, pungent aroma. In this ingenious recipe, the intense piquant flavour of the Idiazábal cheese acts as the perfect foil for the salty ham and tender baby broad beans.

Cuaja de queso Idiazábal sobre habitas salteadas con jamón Ibérico

Idiazábal curd cheese with baby broad beans and Iberian ham

INGREDIENTS (SERVES 4)

1 handful of fresh mint, chopped

2 tablespoons olive oil

100g (3½oz) fresh baby broad
   beans, pods removed

100g (3½oz) Iberian ham or
   serrano ham, chopped

FOR THE CURD CHEESE

300ml (10½fl oz) milk

400g (14oz) Idiazábal cheese,
   grated

300ml (10½fl oz) double cream

7 sheets of leaf gelatine, soaked
   in cold water

1 sifón iSi

toasted spiced bread, to serve
   (optional)

For the curd cheese, pour the milk into a saucepan and bring to boiling point over a medium heat. Then remove from the heat and add the cheese to the hot milk, without stirring. Set aside to infuse and cool for 30 minutes.

When cold, stir in the cream and strain through a sieve into a clean saucepan. Return to the heat and warm gently over a low heat. Add the gelatine and stir until dissolved. Pour into a cream-whipping siphon fitted with 2 nitrous oxide gas cylinders and set aside to cool. Put in the refrigerator to set.

Put the mint in a bowl, cover with olive oil and leave to infuse for 15 minutes.

Blanch the broad beans in a saucepan of boiling water for 5 minutes. Drain off the hot water and cool quickly under cold running water. Then peel the skin off every bean. Transfer to a bowl and toss with a drizzle of mint oil.

Heat 2 tablespoons of olive oil in a frying pan over a medium heat and sauté the ham until it is crisp. Squirt some curd cheese out of the siphon into each of the cocktail glasses, to half fill them. Put 2 teaspoons of the warm sautéed bean and ham mixture on top of the chilled curd and crown with a thin slice of toasted spiced bread, if desired.

WINE TIPS

SPECIAL OCCASION: **Lautus, Guelbenzu, Ribera del Queiles (€€€)**
SUNDAY LUNCH: **Castillo de Monjardín Reserva, Navarra (€€)**
EVERYDAY: **Ochoa Cabernet Sauvignon, Navarra (€)**

Fresh vegetables feature prominently in Navarran cuisine. Much is made of the *piquillo* pepper: a small variety, with a red skin and meaty texture. The *piquillos* are harvested in autumn, roasted over wood fires, then peeled by hand and preserved whole in jars of olive oil, which gives them a unique flavour and texture that can be enjoyed throughout the year.

Alcachofas de Tudela con asado de pimiento de piquillo de Lodosa y borrajas al carbón

Tudela artichokes with chargrilled peppers and borrajas

INGREDIENTS (SERVES 4)

8 fresh baby globe artichokes

juice of 1 lemon

salt

250g (9oz) fresh parsley

200g (7oz) *borrajas* (a green leafy vegetable similar to Swiss chard), shredded

200g (7oz) jar of *Pimientos del piquillo* (*piquillo* peppers)

1 tablespoon olive oil

100g (3¹/₂oz) flaked almonds, cut into slivers

pinch of *polvo de humo* (hickory smoked powder)

To prepare the artichokes, cut through the equator with a sharp knife and throw away the tops. Pull out the tough leaves around the base and discard. Carefully peel the stem and trim off all the remaining tough outer green leaves around the sides and base until left with only the white part. Dig out the inedible hairy choke in the middle with a spoon and discard. (Artichoke hearts go black very quickly when peeled and exposed to air. To prevent discolouration, pour half the lemon juice into a bowl of cold water and keep dunking the artichoke in the acidulated water.)

To cook the artichokes, put the hearts, with stalks attached, into a stainless saucepan, cover with water and add the lemon juice, salt and parsley. Bring to the boil over a high heat, then remove from the heat and allow to cool in the water.

Blanch the *borrajas* in a saucepan of lightly salted boiling water, then cool quickly under a running tap. Drain well in a colander and set aside.

Drain the olive oil from the *piquillos*. Remove the seeds and stems, place in a food processor and blend to a smooth purée.

Heat the olive oil in a frying pan over a medium heat. Sauté the almonds until lightly browned and mix in the *borrajas* and *polvo de humo*.

Arrange 2 artichoke hearts on each plate, with the stalks pointing upward. Pile the smoky almonds and *borrajas* on top and spoon a little pepper purée to one side.

WINE TIPS

SPECIAL OCCASION: **Conde de la Vega Reserva, Palacio de la Vega, Navarra (€€€)**
SUNDAY LUNCH: **Príncipe de Viana 1423, Navarra (€€)**
EVERYDAY: **Señorío de Sarría Reserva, Navarra (€)**

Another boldly flavoured cheese made from unpasteurized sheep's milk is produced in the Roncal Valley region of Navarra. It's a hard, ivory-coloured cheese with holes, which has a creamy texture and a strong, slightly spicy taste. This recipe was designed to highlight its unique flavour. Eating fresh asparagus with Roncal cheese is a truly inspired and mouthwatering combination.

Espárragos blancos en tempura con mayonesa de queso de Roncal

White asparagus tempura with Roncal cheese mayonnaise

INGREDIENTS (SERVES 4)

20 spears white asparagus

200g (7oz) Roncal cheese, Manchego, or any other hard sheep's cheese, finely grated

FOR THE TEMPURA BATTER

30g (1oz) easy-blend dried yeast

100g (3½oz) plain flour

1 teaspoon salt

1 teaspoon caster sugar

500ml (18fl oz) warm water

FOR THE MAYONNAISE

3 eggs

2 egg yolks

1 teaspoon Dijon mustard

300ml (10½fl oz) sunflower oil

75ml (2½fl oz) olive oil

1 teaspoon Sherry wine vinegar

1 sifón iSi

olive oil for frying

Make the tempura batter by combining all the ingredients, except the water, in a large bowl and mix well. Stir in the water and leave in a warm place to ferment until required.

For the mayonnaise, beat all the ingredients together until the mixture has a thick texture. Put in the cream-whipping siphon fitted with 2 nitrous oxide gas cylinders and set aside in a cool place.

Cut the asparagus spears in half lengthways. Bring a large saucepan of water to the boil, drop in the asparagus and blanch briefly for 2 minutes. Remove from the water, cool under cold running water and dry well on a clean tea towel.

Heat plenty of olive oil in a large saucepan or wok and cook over a high heat until a drop of batter starts frying as soon as it hits the hot oil. Dip each asparagus spear in the tempura batter and fry for about 60 seconds until golden and crisp. Carefully remove from the olive oil and drain on kitchen paper.

Pipe the mayonnaise from the siphon into a bowl and fold in the cheese.

Arrange 10 asparagus spears on each plate. Serve with a bowl of the cheesy mayonnaise froth.

WINE TIPS

SPECIAL OCCASION: **Colección 125 Tinto Reserva, Chivite, Navarra (€€€)**

SUNDAY LUNCH: **Barón de Magaña, Bodegas Viña Magaña, Navarra (€€)**

EVERYDAY: **Azul, Guelbenzu, Ribera del Queiles (€)**

The neighbouring Basque Country helps to account for the abundance and freshness of the seafood that plays such a prominent role in Navarran cuisine. One of the most popular items is baby squid, which is eaten everywhere in the taverns and restaurants, accompanied by local wines. In this recipe, the fresh black pasta and the aroma of truffles produces a dish that tastes as good as it looks.

Lasaña de chipirones con aceite de trufa y majado de cebollino y aguacate

Baby squid lasagne with truffle oil and avocado and spring onion salsa

INGREDIENTS (SERVES 4)

8 sheets of fresh lasagne made with squid ink

3 tablespoons olive oil

1 teaspoon salt

32 baby squid

2 avocados, finely chopped

5 spring onions, finely sliced

4 teaspoons squid ink

3 tablespoons sunflower oil

1 onion, thinly sliced

2 tablespoons truffle oil

Put plenty of water in a saucepan, add 1 tablespoon of olive oil and the salt, and bring to the boil over a high heat. Cook the pasta for about 5 minutes.

Put the cleaned squid under a medium grill for 15 minutes until browned, turning halfway through the cooking time.

Meanwhile, mix the avocados, spring onions and 1 tablespoon olive oil together to make a salsa.

Pour the squid ink into a bowl and whisk in the sunflower oil to make a vinaigrette.

Heat the remaining olive oil in a frying pan and fry the onion until very crunchy.

Lay a sheet of lasagne on each plate, top with 8 baby squid, a little of the crunchy onion, and some avocado and spring onion salsa. Pour a drizzle of truffle oil on top and cover with another sheet of pasta. Finish off with a little more avocado and spring onion salsa, some strands of crunchy onion and the remaining squid. Drizzle the squid ink vinaigrette around the plate.

WINE TIPS

SPECIAL OCCASION: **Colección 125 Blanco Reserva, Chivite, Navarra (€€€)**
SUNDAY LUNCH: **Palacio de Otazu Fermentado en Barrica, Navarra (€€)**
EVERYDAY: **Monte Cristo, Camilo Castilla, Navarra (€)**

Wines of Navarra

The DO Navarra was established in 1958, but it's only since the late 1980s that the region has really started to makes its name known in the outside world. Historically, Navarra grew Garnacha grapes and made rosado (rosé) wine, even though its best wines have always been red. In the 1970s and 1980s, importers in other countries (notably the UK) started to market the red wines of Navarra as being 'very similar to Rioja but quite a bit cheaper', but this didn't help profitability or investment, either.

The largest and oldest (1647) bodega in the region is Julián Chivite; even in the mid-1980s it accounted for more than 50 per cent of all wine exported from Navarra. The 1990s, however, saw a big increase in inward investment, partly due to the support provided by the *conseja regulador*, or regulatory body, which had liberalized the regulations and made it possible to grow a wide range of grapes and experiment with more modern styles of winemaking. As a result, although Garnacha and Tempranillo are still prominent, the vineyard now has Cabernet Sauvignon and Merlot, with Chardonnay and Moscatel for whites. The last has achieved cult status in recent years and a number of bodegas (notably Camilo Castilla, Ochoa and Chivite) are turning out world-class examples of sweet wines made from it, some of which are lightly fortified.

Navarra's main strength, however, is its reds and, to a lesser extent whites. Garnacha is still the most widely planted grape, but you're as likely to find wines made from 100 per cent Cabernet Sauvignon, Cabernet-Merlot mixes and even the odd Pinot Noir -- there are some three dozen experimental varieties being trialled at any one time. Red wines that seem to do best in international tastings tend to be about two-thirds Tempranillo and a third Cabernet and/or Merlot. For whites, Chardonnay has made its home here with a vengeance and some of Navarra's finest whites are, typically, barrel-fermented with anything up to a year in the barrel afterwards. A cheaper option is to blend in some Viura: the more there is, the lower the price. And, of course, good old rosado hasn't gone away.

Garnacha turns out delicious, easy-drinking wines made by the sangrado method, in which the grapes are crushed and left on the skins for anything from a few hours to a day and the juice is run off when the winemaker decides the colour is right.

NB: the south-eastern part of Navarra produces wines under the DOCa Rioja and these are discussed in the chapter on La Rioja.

OTHER WINES
VdlT Ribera del Queiles

A cross-border VdlT area, following the tiny River Queiles, which flows into Navarra from Aragón (*see* Aragón, page 30). It was created as a result of the Guelbenzu family's desire to make a wine under their own name from grapes grown on both sides of the border. This is forbidden under DO regulations, so they withdrew from the Navarra DO in 2003 and started calling their wine by this name. It was confirmed officially in 2005, even though they are still the only producer.

OTHER DRINKS

Pacharán, or *Patxaran*, is an anis-flavoured spirit made all over northern Spain, but it originated in Navarra and has ties with other flavoured spirits made in southern France, going back to the days of the Kingdom of Navarre. Anis is not the only ingredient; the main fruit controlled by the *consejo regulador* is sloes, which are macerated in pure alcohol for anything from one to eight months. The anis is added before and after the process, and many producers have secret ingredients that they add to give the final flavour. Pacharán may be anything from clear to pink to almost red in colour, depending on the length of maceration of the sloes, and it may be sweet, dry or anything in between. Typically 25 to 30 per cent alcohol, it's drunk as an *aperitivo* or a *digestivo*, depending on the sweetness or personal preference.

Main Bodegas

(listed in alphabetical order), PRODUCER NAME; town/village; web/E-mail address; best wines (r = red, w = white, p = pink) A star (*) indicates particularly good quality.

ARTADI; Artazu; www.artadi.com; Artazuri (r), Santa Cruz de Artazu (r)*

CAMILO CASTILLA; Corella; www.bodegascamilocastilla.com; Capricho de Goya (sweet w)*, Moscatel Montecristo (sweet w)*

CASTILLO DE MONJARDÍN; Villamayor de Monjardín; www.monjardin.es; Castillo de Monjardín (r, w)

IRACHE; Ayegui; www.irache.com; Castillo Irache (r)

JULIÁN CHIVITE; Cintruenigo; www.bodegaschivite.com; Colección 125 (r, w)*, Gran Feudo Viñas Viejas (r)*

LUÍS GURPEGUI MUGA; San Adrián; Monty Ory (r)

NEKEAS; Añorbe; www.nekeas.com; Izar de Nekeas (r)

OCHOA; Olite; www.bodegasochoa.com; Ochoa (r, w), Dulce (sweet w)*

OTAZU; Echaurri; www.otazu.com; Palacio de Otazu (r)

PRÍNCIPE DE VIANA; Murchante; www.principedeviana.com; Príncipe de Viana (r, p, w)

SARRÍA; Puente la Reina; www.bodegadesarria.com; Señorío de Sarria (r, w)

VINÍCOLA DE NAVARRA; Tiebas; www.domecqbodegas.com; Castillo de Javier (r), Las Campanas Reserva (r)

P aís Vasco, or the Basque Country in English (*Euskadi* in Basque), is an area famous for heavy industry, shipbuilding and exports, and it remains one of the most prosperous regions in the whole of Europe. Historically, the area covered land in France (Gascony) and Spain, and under the Franco régime, Basque language and culture were suppressed. Since the constitution of 1978, however, it has been an autonomous community within Spain. There are three provinces: Vizcaya (Bizkaia) on the north coast, whose capital is Bilbao (Bilbo); Guipúzcoa (Gipuzkoa) to the east along the coast to the French border, whose capital is San Sebastián (Donostia); and to the south behind the Cantabrian Mountains, Álava (Araba), whose capital is Vitoria (Gasteiz).

LOCAL SPECIALITIES

Food is central to Basque life and Basque cookery is reckoned among the best in the world. There's an understandable emphasis on high-quality ingredients: fish, meat, cheese, fruit and vegetables are produced

País Vasco

here in abundance and at very high-quality levels. In addition to the national system of *denominaciones*, the Basque government awards its own 'Eusko' label to quality products.

Idiazábal is the region's most famous cheese, made from the milk of Lacha and Carranzana sheep. Traditionally smoked over beech wood, it also comes unsmoked, and ages well, becoming crumbly when mature. *Pollo de Caserío Vasco* (Basque farmhouse chicken) is a protected breed of fowl that lives a free-range life, is fed mainly on maize and is claimed to represent the real taste of old country-style chicken. *Cordero lechal del País Vasco* is milk-fed baby lamb of the same breeds that produce *idiazábal* cheese, only available seasonally; *carne de vacuno del País Vasco* is beef from cattle from certified herds, available only through selected butchers.

Fruit and vegetables abound, with protected status for the organic *patata* (potato) *de Álava*, the long green peppers of Gernika (*pimiento de Gernika*), *guindillas* (chilli peppers) *de Ibarra* and *tomate de calidad del País Vasco* – farm-grown tomatoes with a unique, traditional taste. There are three categories for haricot beans alone: *alubia pinta Alavesa, alubia de Gernika* and *alubia de Tolosa*, and the *Euskal Baserri* label guarantees farm produce as locally grown to strict standards.

With such a long coastline, fishing has always been a primary industry, and the local tuna (*bonito del norte y cimarrón*), traditionally fished with rod and line, is also protected, as is the local honey. The Basques take their food very seriously.

Fortunately, looks aren't everything where the large-scaled scorpionfish is concerned: it may be one of the ugliest fish in the world, but it tastes delicious. In Spain, it's known by various names: in Castile and Asturias, they call it *escarpena*; in Cataluña, *cap roig*; and in the Basque Country, *kabrarroka*. In this recipe, the scorpionfish's incredible flavour really shines through, while its appearance is cleverly disguised.

Pastel de cabracho

Red scorpionfish cake

INGREDIENTS (SERVES 4)

500g (1lb 2oz) scorpionfish, scaled

1 tablespoon butter

2 tablespoons dried natural
    breadcrumbs

2 large tomatoes

50ml (2fl oz) olive oil

pinch of salt

pinch of sugar

4 eggs

salt and white pepper to taste

300g (10½oz) filo pastry, cut into
    triangular pieces

30g (1oz) butter, melted

GARNISH

thin strands of leek, deep fried

edible flower petals, from
    nasturtiums and marigolds
    (optional)

Put the fish in a saucepan, cover with water and bring to the boil over a medium heat. Cook just long enough so that the fish flakes off the bones and skin easily. Set aside to cool.

Preheat the oven to 200°C (400°F, gas mark 6). Grease a 900g (2lb) non-stick loaf tin with butter and sprinkle breadcrumbs over the sides.

Purée the tomatoes. Heat the olive oil in a frying pan and cook the tomatoes with the salt and sugar over a low heat for 10 minutes. Allow to cool.

Whisk the eggs until fluffy and pale, fold in the fish and tomato sauce, and season with salt and pepper. Pour into the prepared tin.

Sit the baking dish in a deep roasting tin and pour in enough hot water to come three-quarters of the way up the sides. Then carefully put in the oven for 30 minutes. Remove from the oven and set aside to cool. Turn the oven down to 180°C (350°F, gas mark 4).

Brush the filo pastry triangles with butter and lay on a baking tray. Bake in the oven for about 3 minutes until golden and crisp.

Turn the fish cake out of the loaf tin onto a chopping board and cut into slices, about 2cm (¾in) thick. Arrange 2 slices on each plate, accompanied by some filo pastry crisps. Garnish with the crisp leek and edible flower petals, if desired.

WINE TIPS

SPECIAL OCCASION: **Organza, Señorío de San Vicente, Rioja (€€€)**
SUNDAY LUNCH: **Blanco Fernández de Piérola, Rioja Alavesa (€€)**
EVERYDAY: **Axpe, José Antonio Bilbao, Bizkaiko Txakolina (€)**

Duck is now trendy in Spain. In addition to its tasty, succulent meat, the liver is used in many elegant recipes in the Basque Country. Here, the combination of cherries, almonds and rose petals produces a fragrant dish, which bombards the senses with a plethora of aromas and colours.

Foie asado sobre cerezas con emulsión de almendras y sal de rosas

Roasted duck's liver on cherries with rose-scented almond cream

INGREDIENTS (SERVES 4):

FOR THE ALMOND CREAM
50g (1³/₄oz) almond paste
500g (1lb 2oz) blanched almonds, chopped
200ml (7fl oz) milk
1 garlic clove
Sherry wine vinegar
olive oil

FOR THE DUCK'S LIVER
1 fresh duck's liver
8 large fresh juicy red cherries, stoned and halved

GARNISH
sea salt flakes
50g (1³/₄oz) dried rose petals
sprigs of fresh marjoram

Put the almond paste, almonds, milk and garlic in a food processor and blend to a cream. Add a little vinegar to adjust the sweetness and olive oil to correct the consistency. Pour into a bowl and keep in the refrigerator until needed.

Preheat the oven to 180°C (350°F, gas mark 4). Put the duck's liver under a hot grill for 2 minutes, then finish cooking in the oven for another 2 or 3 minutes until cooked through.

Arrange 4 halves of cherry in the centre of each plate. Put a quarter of the hot duck's liver on top. Garnish with sea salt flakes, rose petals and sprigs of fresh marjoram. Serve with the almond cream.

WINE TIPS

SPECIAL OCCASION: **Barón de Chirel, Marqués de Riscal, Rioja Alavesa (€€€)**
SUNDAY LUNCH: **Conde de Valdemar Crianza, Rioja Alavesa (€€)**
EVERYDAY: **Pérez Irazu Joven, Rioja Alavesa (€)**

Fish and seafood soup is a mainstay of Spanish cuisine. Per head of population, Spain is the second-largest consumer of fish in the world. Each region has its own recipes, but those from the Basque Country are probably the best. To make a seafood soup requires fresh and varied ingredients, and enormous patience. The result is usually a magnificent feast, and well worth the time and effort involved.

Sopa de mariscos y pescado
Traditional fish and seafood soup

INGREDIENTS (SERVES 4)

4kg (8lb 12oz) bones and heads from hake and monkfish

3kg (6lb 8oz) lobster, prawn and langoustine heads

60ml (2¼fl oz) oil

1 carrot, diced

1 leek, finely chopped

1 large onion, finely chopped

2 garlic cloves, finely chopped

2 ripe tomatoes, skinned and chopped

100g (3½oz) bread, sliced

250ml (9fl oz) tomato sauce

125ml (4fl oz) brandy

275ml (9½fl oz) white wine

FOR THE GARNISH

2 tablespoons olive oil

1 garlic clove, chopped

200g (7oz) various fish flesh (hake, angler fish, grouper)

4 prawns

4 langoustines

8 clams

240 ml (8½fl oz) brandy

1 tablespoon chopped parsley

To make a quantity of fish stock, put half the fish bones and heads in a large saucepan, cover with water, bring to the boil and simmer over a medium heat for 30 minutes, then strain.

Heat 2 tablespoons olive oil in a large saucepan and sauté the remaining fish bones and heads and the shellfish heads in batches. Combine all the prepared vegetables, except the tomatoes, in a bowl and drizzle with 1 tablespoon olive oil; set aside.

To start making the soup, heat 1 tablespoon of olive oil in a large clean saucepan. Add the tomatoes and simmer for 15 or 20 minutes. Add the sliced bread, sauté, and then add the tomato sauce.

Leave to cook for 20 minutes, then add the brandy. Once reduced by half, add the white wine. When the liquid has reduced by half again add the prepared vegetables and leave everything to cook together for 15 minutes.

After this time, add the fish stock and simmer over a low heat for 50 minutes. Leave the soup to cool a little before pouring into a food processor and blending until completely smooth.

Now make the garnish. In a frying pan, heat the olive oil over a high heat, add the garlic and sauté briefly, without browning. Then add the fish pieces, prawns, langoustines and clams, and sauté for 5 minutes. Drench in brandy, heat and flambé.

Ladle some soup into each bowl and arrange a good selection of the sautéed fish and shellfish on top as a garnish. Finish with a sprinkling of chopped parsley.

WINE TIPS

SPECIAL OCCASION: **Remelluri Blanco, Rioja Alavesa (€€€)**
SUNDAY LUNCH: **Cosme Palacio Blanco, Palacio, Rioja Alavesa (€€)**
EVERYDAY: **Txakolina, Txomin Etxaniz, Getariako Txakolina (€)**

Wines of País Vasco

This far north, white grapes ripen more readily than red. This, coupled with the readily available seafood, has resulted in the local wines (all called Txakoli/Chacolí) being predominantly white. The main grape is the Hondarribi Zuri, which is not found anywhere else in the world, and the wines are light and very fresh, with crisp acidity and sometimes a residual hint of sparkle to tickle the tongue.

NB: the southern part of the province of Álava produces wines under the DOCa Rioja, and these are discussed in the chapter on La Rioja.

DO GETARIAKO TXAKOLINA/CHACOLÍ DE GUETARIA
The first of the Txakoli areas to be delimited, in 1990, it covers an area of land around the coastal towns of Getaria and Zarautz, inland as far as Aia in the province of Gipuzkoa (Guipúzcoa).

DO BIZKAIKO TXAKOLINA/CHACOLÍ DE VIZCAYA
A widely spread area from the coast, well inland and completely surrounding the city of Bilbao. Many plantations are very small indeed, including some tiny plots within the city itself.

DO ARABAKO TXAKOLINA/CHACOLÍ DE ÁLAVA
The smallest and most recent (2002) of the areas, in the province of Álava, mainly around the town of Amurrio. There are only three bodegas and one of them, Arabako Txakolina, is responsible for more than 90 per cent of all production.

OTHER DRINKS
Along with its north-coast neighbours, the Basque Country has a thriving *sidra* (cider) industry, particularly in Gipuzkoa, which started making cider on a commercial scale in the 1930s. They describe it as 'hard' or 'natural' cider and it's made with wild apples grown in the woodland orchards of the province. The cider-maker can choose from a number of varieties, including Geza, Miña and Moko for bitterness; Manttoni, Txalaka, Urtebi txiki and Urtebi haundi for acidity; and Mozolua and Patzoloa for sweetness. Every *sidreria* has a different formula, of course, but chemical additions are forbidden. The *sidra de Gipuzkoa* even has its own specially designed bottle. Although they recommend holding it at least 30cm (12in) above the glass for pouring to aerate the cider, they don't demand the physical contortions favoured by the *Asturianos.*

Main Bodegas
(listed in alphabetical order), PRODUCER NAME; town/village; web/E-mail address; best wines (r = red, w = white)
A star (*) indicates particularly good quality.

DO GETARIAKO TXAKOLINA/CHACOLÍ DE GUETARIA
www.getariakotxakolina.com

TALAI-BERRI; Zarautz; www.talaiberri.com; Talai-Berri (w)

TXOMIN ETXANIZ; Getaria; www.txominetxaniz.com; Txomin Etxaniz (w)

DO BIZKAIKO TXAKOLINA/CHACOLÍ DE VIZCAYA
www.bizkaikotxakolina.org

BERROJA; Muxica; www.bodegaberroja.com; Agirrebeko (w)

ITSASMENDI; Gernika; www.bodegasitsasmendi.com; Itsasmendi (w), Aihen (w)

ITURRIALDE; Mungia; www.gorkaizagirre.com; Aretxondo (w), Egia Enea (w)*

DO ARABAKO TXAKOLINA/CHACOLÍ DE ÁLAVA
www.txakolidealava.com

ARABAKO TXAKOLINA; Amurrio; www.arabakotxakolina.com; Xarmant (w)

BELDIU; Llodio; www.beldiu.com; Beldiu (w)

V alencia is Spain's third city and biggest wine port; the export culture runs deep among the major bodegas, which supply a good deal of Europe's supermarket trade. Historically, the region is part of 'greater Cataluña', and the local language, Valenciano, is a dialect of Catalan – road and direction signs are careful to spell it as València as well as in the Castilian style. The city, however, is extremely cosmopolitan, thanks to its seafaring and trading culture, and most European languages can be heard. The architect Santiago Calatrava was born here, and shot to fame as the designer of the Olympic stadium in Barcelona in 1992.

Valencia

In the 21st century, he returned home and helped to create the magnificent City of Arts and Sciences, which revitalized the central part of the city. The region consists of three provinces: Castelló de la Plana in the north, Valencia in the centre and Alicante to the south, all of them along the east coast.

LOCAL SPECIALITIES

Oranges are what most people think of when Valencia is mentioned; indeed, the Valencia oval is the most important variety in the world of orange cultivation. But it's not all citrus fruit: *kaki de la Ribera del Xúquer* is a variety of persimmon, mainly grown in Carlet and l'Alcudia, about 40km (25 miles) south of the city. *Nisperos de Callosa d'en Sarrià* are medlars grown about 20km (12 miles) inland from Calpe on the Alicante coast. *Uva de Mesa Embolsada Vinalopó* are table grapes ripened inside transparent bags to protect them from insects and fungal diseases in an area near the Murcian border with Alicante, about 40km (25 miles) west of Elche, which itself is famous for melons, and *cerezas de la montana de Alicante* are cherries grown in the highlands of northern Alicante and southern Valencia provinces.

One of Valencia's main crops is rice, with the biggest paddy fields in Europe and exports to China, among other countries. *Paella* was first made, according to legend, in Dénia in Alicante. *Chufa de València* are tiger nuts (which are also turned into tiger-nut milk) grown just north of the city of Valencia; and the province of Castelló de la Plana is famous for its artichokes: *alcachofa de Benicarló* has been grown around the town for several centuries.

Elsewhere the region is as rich in local produce as the rest of Spain, with marks of quality for honey, olive oil, spicy pork products, including *longaniza* (flavoured with chillis and/or spices) and *morcilleta* (black pudding, sometimes with onions and/or peppers). *Cordero Guirro* is a breed of sheep unique to the Valencia region.

In Valencia, there have always been numerous vegetable gardens, as well as chickens, rabbits and rice paddies: it was only a matter of time before all these ingredients came together in a single dish, the *paella*, which is now a culinary icon in Spanish culture. There are many ways of assembling a *paella*, but the traditional version stays loyal to the local ingredients, plus saffron and a selection of seafood.

Paella Valenciana

Paella, Valencia-style

INGREDIENTS (SERVES 4)

2 tablespoons olive oil

450g (1lb) rabbit meat, cut into small pieces

600g (1lb 5oz) chicken breast, cut into small pieces

280g (10oz) fine green beans, cut into 2cm (3/4in) lengths

150g (5 1/2oz) white string beans, cut into 2cm (3/4in) lengths

150g (5 1/2oz) butter beans

100g (3 1/2oz) tomatoes, skinned, deseeded and finely chopped

400g (14oz) short-grain rice

1 tablespoon paprika

pinch of saffron strands

850ml (1 1/2 pint) water

salt and pepper to taste

150g (5 1/2oz) clams, shells on

12 baby octopus

8 baby squid

GARNISH

sprigs of fresh dill

4 king prawns, cooked (optional)

Heat the olive oil in a *paellera* (paella pan) or a very large frying pan, over a medium heat. When the oil is hot, add the rabbit and chicken and sauté until golden brown.

Then add all the chopped beans. Continue to cook the mixture for a further 8 minutes, before adding the tomatoes.

Stir until the mixture dries out a little, then add the rice, paprika, saffron and water to the pan and mix well. Bring to the boil over a medium heat, season with salt and pepper, then add the clams, baby octopus and squid. Reduce the heat and continue to cook, without stirring, for 16–18 minutes, until the rice is tender but not dry.

Spoon some *paella* into each bowl. Garnish with sprigs of fresh dill and a large cooked prawn, if desired.

WINE TIPS

SPECIAL OCCASION: Generación 1, Vicente Gandía, Utiel-Requena (€€€)

SUNDAY LUNCH: Casa Don Ángel Bobal, Vere de Estenas, Utiel-Requena (€€)

EVERYDAY: Almuvedre, Telmo Rodríguez, Alicante (€)

The taverns, *chiringuitos* (refreshment stands) and small bars along the Valencian coast are magnets for hungry bathers, attracted by the appetizing aroma of seafood grilling over hot charcoal. Prawns from the Dénia area are especially famous for their sweet flavour and pinkness. Drizzling a little smoky-scented charcoal oil over this light broth is designed to evoke the magical smell of those open-air grills.

Gambas de Dénia al aceite de carbón

Dénia prawns with charcoal oil

INGREDIENTS (SERVES 4)

2 tablespoons olive oil

1 garlic clove, chopped

1 teaspoon paprika

1 onion, chopped

1 carrot, chopped

1 leek, chopped

1 teaspoon cayenne pepper

2 sprigs of tarragon, chopped

2 sprigs of chervil, chopped

50g (1³/₄oz) prawn shells

3 lobster heads

1kg (2lb 4oz) shrimps

1 tablespoon Cognac

70g (2¹/₂oz) short-grain rice

16 large raw prawns

salt and pepper to taste

FOR THE CHARCOAL OIL

250g (9oz) rice bran

150g (5¹/₂oz) lapsang souchong China tea

2 tablespoons olive oil

fresh herbs, to garnish (optional)

For the stock, heat the olive oil in a large stockpot over a low heat. Sauté the garlic until lightly golden, stir in the paprika, then tip in all the vegetables and sweat until tender but not browned. Mix in the cayenne, tarragon and chervil, and add the prawn shells, lobster heads and shrimps. Sauté over a medium heat until browned. Pour in the Cognac, heat briefly, then flambé.

Pour in the rice, cover with plenty of water and bring to the boil over a medium heat. Then turn down the heat and simmer for 1 hour. Remove the stockpot from the heat, strain the stock through a sieve into a bowl and leave to cool. Season to taste with salt and pepper, and set aside.

For the charcoal oil, toast the rice bran in the oven at 130°C (250°F, gas mark ½), until totally blackened like 'charcoal'. Mix with the tea, which provides the smoky flavour, and blitz to a fine powder in a coffee grinder. Store the powder in a dry, airtight container to preserve the smoky aroma. Just before serving, mix 2 teaspoons of the charcoal powder into the olive oil.

Peel the prawns, removing the tails but leaving the heads on. Rub with olive oil, sprinkle with a little salt and place under a hot grill for about 2 minutes, turning once, until evenly pink all over.

Arrange 4 prawns in the centre of each shallow bowl and pour in a little shellfish stock. Drizzle a few drops of the charcoal oil over the top. Garnish with fresh herbs, if desired.

WINE TIPS

SPECIAL OCCASION: **Verdeval Especial Roble, Vins del Comtat, Comunidad Valenciana (€€€)**
SUNDAY LUNCH: **Verderón, Casa del Pinar, Utiel-Requena (€€)**
EVERYDAY: **Enrique Mendoza Chardonnay, Alicante (€)**

Langostinos from Vinarós hold a special place of honour among the produce of the Levante area. Up to 20cm (8in) long, with a bright pink colour, they are the colourful giants of the prawn world. Their sweet, juicy flesh has always dazzled and beguiled great chefs. When combined with the juice of local oranges and rice, the king prawns more than live up to their reputation for being absolutely delicious.

Emulsión de erizo de mar con arroz de langostinos de Vinarós y sofrito de naranja

Sea urchins with king prawns, rice and orange

INGREDIENTS (SERVES 4)

4 tablespoons olive oil
1 onion, finely chopped
1 leek, finely sliced
2 tomatoes, skinned, deseeded
    and chopped
200g (7oz) oranges
250g (9oz) monkfish, cut into
    small pieces
roe of 2 sea urchins, sliced
    (remove the spines, wash the
    shells and save for later plus
    6 more spineless washed sea
    urchin shells)
300g (10¹/₂oz) short-grain rice
1 litre (1³/4 pint) fish stock
8 raw king prawns, shelled
8 small clams, shells on
salt and pepper to taste
handful of fresh mint leaves,
    finely chopped, to garnish

Heat 2 tablespoons of the olive oil in a large saucepan and sauté the onion and leek until golden. Then add the tomatoes and cook for 4 minutes.

Squeeze the juice from the oranges and add to the saucepan with the fish. Cook for 2 minutes, then stir in the sea urchin roe until covered with orange juice.

Tip the rice and fish stock into the saucepan and simmer over a medium heat for 10 minutes. Then mix in the king prawns and clams and cook for a further 3 minutes. Stir gently with a wooden spoon, mix in the remaining olive oil, season with salt and pepper and set aside to rest.

Place 2 spineless sea urchin shells on each plate. Fill all the shells with rice and fish and serve with 2 king prawns and 2 clams per portion. Garnish with a light sprinkling of fresh mint.

WINE TIPS

SPECIAL OCCASION: **Casta Divi Monte Diva, Gutiérrez de la Vega, Alicante (€€€)**
SUNDAY LUNCH: **Las Tres, Chozas Carrascal, Utiel-Requena (€€)**
EVERYDAY: **Murviedro Blanco, Valencia (€)**

Spain has the largest area of date palms under cultivation in Europe. Introduced by the Berbers of the Sahara, their splendid legacy is best seen in the magnificent *Palmeral de Elche*, where 200,000 date palms grow in a series of orchards and produce 8,000 tonnes of dates a year. The sweet, luscious, golden fruit harmonizes perfectly with the nuts and chocolate in this recipe.

Pastel de guianduja con chocolate y dátiles dulces de Elche en texturas frías y calientes

Hot and cold hazelnut praline cake with chocolate and Elche dates

INGREDIENTS (SERVES 4)

FOR THE *GUIANDUJA*
85g (3oz) caster sugar
115g (4oz) toasted hazelnuts, chopped
175g (6oz) milk chocolate

FOR THE CHOCOLATE MOUSSE
175ml (6fl oz) whipping cream
175g (6oz) plain chocolate
150ml (5fl oz) double cream
pinch of Chinese five spice powder

FOR THE *GUIANDUJA* MOUSSE
175ml (6fl oz) double cream
1 sheet of leaf gelatine, soaked
250g (9oz) *guianduja* (*see* above)
350g (12oz) whipping cream
4 dates, thinly sliced

FOR THE CHOCOLATE GLAZE
125ml (4fl oz) water
75ml (2¹/₂fl oz) liquid glucose
4 sheets of leaf gelatine, soaked
200g (7oz) dark chocolate

For the *guianduja*, put the sugar and hazelnuts in a small heavy-based saucepan over a medium heat until the sugar turns golden brown. Remove from the heat and stir to coat the hazelnuts. Line a baking tray with baking parchment and carefully pour the hot nutty caramel onto the tray. Spread out thinly and leave to cool until brittle. Smash 250g (9oz) of the hazelnut praline into a rough mixture (*not* a powder) in a food processor. Set the rest of the sheet aside. Break the chocolate into a bowl and melt over a saucepan of simmering water. Stir in the crushed praline and set aside.

For the chocolate mousse, pour the whipping cream into a saucepan and bring to the boil. Break the plain chocolate into a bowl and pour in the hot cream. Stir well until the chocolate has melted. When the chocolate cream has cooled, but is still slightly warm, stir in the double cream and five spice powder. Half fill four 40g (1¹/₂oz) ingot moulds (mini individual loaf tins would be suitable) with the spicy chocolate cream and set aside to cool, before putting in the refrigerator to set.

For the *guianduja* mousse, bring the cream to the boil in a saucepan and stir in the gelatine until dissolved. Stir into the *guianduja* (*see* above) and mix well. When the mixture has cooled slightly, stir in the whipping cream, pour into the half-filled moulds and top with the dates. Allow to cool, before putting in the refrigerator to set.

For the chocolate glaze, bring the water and glucose to the boil in a small saucepan, then remove from the heat. Stir in the gelatine until dissolved. Break the chocolate into a bowl, then pour the hot sweet water over the chocolate.

Lay 4 pieces of the remaining *guianduja* on a wire cake-cooling rack. Turn out the chilled mousses and place on top of the *guianduja*. Top with chocolate glaze.

WINE TIPS
SPECIAL OCCASION: **Dolç de Mendoza, Enrique Mendoza, Alicante (€€€)**
SUNDAY LUNCH: **Casta Diva Miel, Gutiérrez de la Vega, Alicante (€€)**
EVERYDAY: **Fusta Nova, Vicente Gandía, Utiel-Requena (€)**

Wines of Valencia

Because of the region's focus on exports, particularly of supermarket wines, it's hard to put a style on the wines of Valencia. The main red grapes are the Monastrell and the Bobal, but with increasing amounts of Tempranillo, Cabernet Sauvignon, *et al*; the main white is the Merseguera, which turns out pleasant but unexceptional everyday wines. The terrain ranges from sea level to about 625m (2,0450ft), so there's a range of microclimates for those bodegas prepared to do more than churn out millions of bottles for the mass market. Bobal, formerly seen only as a grape for bulk wines, is turning out to be a very promising grape in the right hands, and several of the more forward-looking bodegas have been experimenting with low-yielding older vines with some considerable success.

Monastrell has been rehabilitated here and is now seen as a real contender for quality wines rather than just a base for blending. Most reds from Alicante are based on this, with Tempranillo and Bobal (especially in Utiel-Requena) a close second. There is some white wine made from Chardonnay, and a few bodegas are working with Merlot and Syrah. The Valencia DO is also a centre for sweet wines made from Malvasía, Moscatel and Pedro Ximénez, usually singly but occasionally in blends. These are some of the best-value sweet wines from Spain

DO ALICANTE

The southernmost DO of the region, with two subzones: one on the coast north of Calpe, the other around and west of Alicante city. They grow Monastrell, Garnacha and Bobal for reds, Merseguera and Moscatel for whites.

DO UTIEL-REQUENA

The furthest inland, next door to the Manchuela DO (Murcia). Bobal is the chief grape, but Tempranillo is second and there is work with Cabernet Sauvignon and Syrah. Vineyards range from 600–900m (1,969–2,953ft) so there is potential here for excellent wines, yet to be fully realized.

DO VALENCIA

This is divided into three subzones, with vineyards from 200m to 625m (656–2,050ft) growing mainly Monastrell and Garnacha for reds and Merseguera for whites. The 'Moscatel de Valencia' area for sweet wines is immediately west of the city itself.

OTHER WINES

Valencia has had a number of country-wine areas, including Benniarés and Lliber-Javea (both in Alicante), many of which are now unofficial. The only two currently registered are these:

VdlT Castelló In Castelló de la Plana, this area was created in 2001 and grows Bobal, Garnacha, Tempranillo and others for reds, and Chardonnay, Malvasia and others for whites. The wines are not well known outside the area.

VdlT Terrerazo This is, perhaps, an example of a high-profile bodega winning its own little VdlT classification (*see* Guelbenzu, page 168). The bodega below has resolutely refused to join the Utiel-Requena DO, in spite of being within the area and working with the Bobal grape.

Other bodegas have chosen not to belong to any of the official wine areas. The most enduring is in Alicante.

OTHER DRINKS

With a well-developed wine-based culture, it was inevitable that the Valencia region should have a wide range of alcoholic drinks. These include *anis paloma de monrote del Cid*, an anis spirit made about 20km (12 miles) west of Alicante; *aperitivo café de Alcoy* is an infused coffee liqueuer made in Alcot, about 60km (37 miles) north of Alicante; *cantueso Alicantino* is a unique, thyme-based liqueur, made in the province of Alicante and aged in oak; and *herbero de la Sierra de Mariola* is a herbal infusion from the Sierra de Mariola National Park in Alicante.

By far the most widespread wine-based drink, however, is *fondillón*, made mainly around Monóvar, about 40km (25 miles) west of the city of Alicantc. Overripe Monastrell grapes (which may also be sun-dried) are fermented and may achieve up to 16 per cent alcohol by volume, after which they are mixed with older wines and allowed to mature. Good *fondillón* has a warm, nutty character, a hint of acidity and a generous, silky finish, and is much in demand as an after-dinner drink.

Main Bodegas

(listed in alphabetical order), PRODUCER NAME; town/village; web/E-mail address; best wines (r = red, w = white)
A star (*) indicates particularly good quality.

DO ALICANTE
www.crdo-alicante.org

ENRIQUE MENDOZA; Alfaz del Pi; www.bodegasmendoza.com; Enrique Mendoza (r)*, Dolç de Mendoza (sweet r)*

GUTIÉRREZ DE LA VEGA; Parcent; www.castadiva.es; Casta Diva (sweet w)*

TELMO RODRÍGUEZ; Logroño; cia@fer.es; El Sequé (r)*

DO UTIEL-REQUENA
www.utielrequena.org

CASA DEL PINAR; Venta del Moro; www.casadelpinar.com; Casa del Pinar (r)*

VICENTE GANDÍA; Chiva; www.gandiawines.com; Hoya de Cadenas (r), Generación 1 (r)*

DO VALENCIA
www.vinovalencia.org

BELDA; Fontanars dels Alforins; www.vinsbjb.com; Daniel Belda (r)

MURVIEDRO; Requena; www.murviedro.es; Estrella (sweet w), Los Monteros (r)

VdlT TERRERAZO

MUSTIGUILLO; Las Cuevas de Utiel; mustiguillo@inicia.es; Finca Terrerazo (r), Quincha Corral (r)*

VINS DEL COMTAT; Cocentaina; www.vinsdelcomtat.com; Montcabrer (r), Penya Cadiella Selecció (r)*

Recommended restaurants

(City names within province listings in italics)
The very best restaurants are annotated below with a star.

ANDALUCÍA

Almería city: La Gruta.

Cádiz city: El Faro. **Province:** *Arcos de la Frontera:* El Convento; *Los Barrios:* El Copo; *Jerez de la Frontera:* La Mesa Redonda; *El Puerto de Santa María:* El Faro del Puerto; *Sanlúcar de Barrameda:* Bigote, El Veranillo.

Córdoba city: Almudaína, El Caballo Rojo, Pic-Nic.

Granada city: Chikito, Los Santanderinos. **Province:** *Cenes de la Vega:* Ruta del Veleta.

Huelva city: Farqueo, Las Meigas. **Province:** *Aracena:* José Vicente; *Isla Cristina:* Casa Rufino; *Punta Umbría:* El Paraíso.

Jaén city: Casa Antonio. **Province:** *Baeza:* Juanito; *Cazorla:* La Sarga.

Málaga city: Adolfo, Café de Paris. **Province:** *Churriana:* La Cónsula (a highly regarded catering college); *Estepona:* La Alcaría de Ramos; *Fuengirola:* El Higuerón; *Marbella:* La Hacienda, El Lago, Ruperto de Nola, Santiago; *El Palo:* Mamé.

Sevilla city: Egaña Oriza, Taberna de Alabardero. **Province:** *Sanlúcar la Mayor:* La Alquería.

ARAGÓN

Huesca city: Lillas Pastia, Las Torres, Venta del Sotón. **Province:** *Barbastro:* Flor; *Hecho:* Gaby-Casa Blasquico; *Jaca:* La Cocina Aragonesa, Lilium; *Aínsa:* Bodegas del Sobrabre, Bodegón de Mallacan, Callizo; *Panticosa:* Lago.

Teruel city: La Menta, La Tierreta. **Province:** *Tramacastilla:* El Batán; *Cantavieja:* Buj.

Zaragoza city: El Cachirulo, Gayarre, Goyesco, La Ontina, Txalupa. **Province:** *Cariñena:* La Rebótica; *Villanueva de Gallego:* Sella-La Val d'Onsella.

ASTURIAS

Oviedo: L'Alezna, Casa Conrado, Del Arco, Casa Fermin.

Gijón: Casa Victor, Paladares, Casa Zabala. **Province:** *Arriondas:* El Corral del Indianu; *Avilés:* Real Balneario; *Mareo:* La Solana; *Prendes:* Casa Gerardo; *La Salgar:* Casa Marcial.

THE BALEARIC ISLANDS

Palma de Mallorca: El Jardin de Son Vida, Koldo Royo, Plat d'Or, Porto Pí, Read's. **Province:** *Andratx:* Miramar; *Bunyola:* Ses Porxeres; *Capdepera:* Ses Rotges; *Deià:* El Olivo, Ca'n Ouet; *Pollença:* Cavall Bernat; *Portals Nous:* Tristán; *Sóller:* Béns d'Avall.

CANARY ISLANDS

Lanzarote: *Yaiza:* La Era. **Tenerife:** *Playa de las Américas:* Bahía del Duque, El Patio; *Puerto de la Cruz:* Botánico; *Santa Cruz de Tenerife:* Mencey.

CANTABRIA

Santander: La Cúpula del Rhin, El Puntal, El Serbal. **Province:** *Escalante:* San Román de Escalante; *Ramales de la Victoria:* Río Asón; *Torrelavega:* Los Avellanos; *Villaverde de Pontones:* Cenador de Amós.

CASTILLA Y LEÓN

Ávila province: *Hoyos del Espino:* El Milano Real.

Burgos city: El Ángel, Landa Palace.

León city: Vivaldi. **Province:** *Astorga:* La Peseta.

Palencia city: Casa Lucio. **Province:** *Carrión de los Condes:* Estrella del Bajo Carrión.

Salamanca city: Chez Victor, Victor Gutiérrez.

Segovia city: La Cocina de Segovia, Mesón de Cándido. **Province:** *Cañicosa:* Codex Calixtinus.

Soria city: Rincón de San Juan.

Zamora city: El Rincón de Antonio, Paris. **Province:** *Benavente:* El Ermitano.

CASTILLA-LA MANCHA

Albacete city: Nuestro Bar, Casa Paco. **Province:** *Almansa:* Mesón de Pincelín.

Ciudad Real city: Miami Park. **Province:** *Almagro:* El Corregidor.

Cuenca province: *Las Pedroñeras:* Las Rejas; *Villalba de la Sierra:* Mesón Nelia.

Guadalajara province: *Marchamalo:* La Llaves; *Sigüenza:* Calle Mayor.

Toledo city: La Alacena. **Province:** *Illescas:* El Bohío.

CATALUÑA
Barcelona city: Abac, Alkimia, Caelis, Drolma, Hofman, Jean Luc Figueras, Moo, Neichel, El Raco d'en Freixa, Via Veneto. **Province:** *Arenys de Mar:* Hispania; *Calldetenes:* Can Jubany; *Sant Andreu de Llavaneres:* L'Esguard; *Sant Celoni:* Can Fabes*; *Sant Pol de Mar:* Sant Pau*.
Girona city: El Celler de Can Roca*. **Province:** *Avinyonet de Puigventós:* Mas Pau; *Bolvir de Cerdanya:* Torre del Remei; *Figueres:* Empordà; *Mont-Ras:* La Cuina de Can Pipes; *Olot:* Les Cols; *Pals:* Sa Punta; *Roses:* El Bulli*; *Torrent:* Mas de Torrent; *Tosaa de Mar:* La Cuina de Can Simón; *Vall de Bianya:* Ca l'Enric.
Lleida city: Carballiera. **Province:** *Arties:* Casa Irene; *La Seu d'Urgell:* Tàpies-Hotel; *Peramola:* Can Boix; *Sort:* Fogony.
Tarragona city: Merlot. **Province:** *Cambrils:* Can Bosch, Rincón de Diego.

EXTREMADURA
Badajoz city: Aldebarán.
Province: *Almendral:* Rocamador; *Mérida:* Altair.
Cáceres city: Atrio*.

GALICIA
A Coruña city: Pardo; Playa Club. **Province:** *Santiago de Compostela:* Toñi Vicente; Casa Marcelo.
Ourense city: San Miguel. **Province:** *Santa Baia:* Galileo.
Pontevedra province: *San Salvador de Poio:* Solla; *Sanxenxo:* Taberna de Rotilio.
Lugo city: España. **Province:** *Santa María de Muxa:* La Palloza; *Viveiro:* Nito.

LA RIOJA
Logroño city: Cachetero, Mesón Egües.
La Rioja province: *Ezcaray:* Echaurren; *Haro:* Las Duelas; *San Vicente de la Sonsierra:* Casa Toni.

MADRID
City: La Broche, Casa d'a Troya, El Chaflán, Santceloni, La Terraza del Casino and Zalacaín. **Outside the city:** *Aranjuez:* Casa José; *Humanes de Madrid:* Coque.

MURCIA
Murcia city: Arco, Rincón de Pepe. **Province:** *El Algar:* José-María Los Churrascos; *Santa Cruz:* Hostería Palacete Rural La Seda.

NAVARRA
Pamplona city: Don Pablo, Enekorri, Europa, Hartza, Josetxo, Rodero.
Navarra province: *Cintruenigo:* Maher; *Puente la Reina:* Mesón del Peregrino; *Tafalla:* Túbal.

PAÍS VASCO
Araba/Álava – Vitoria/Gasteiz: Zaldiarán, Ikea, El Portalón.
Araba province: *Lezama:* Bideko; *Llodio:* Palacio de Anuncibai.
Bizkaia/Vizcaya – Bilbao/Bilbo: Guggenheim*, Zortziko, Etxanobe, Goizeko-Kabi.
Bizkaia province: *Foría:* Baserri Maitea; *Galdakao:* Andra Mari.
Gipuzkoa/Guipúzcoa – San Sebastian/Donostia: Akelare*, Arzak*, Miramón Arbelaitz.
Gipuzkoa province: *Bergara/Vergara:* Lasa; *Errenteria/Rentería – Mugaritz*; *Hernani:* Fagollaga; *Hondarribia/Fuenterrabia:* Alameda, Ramón Roteta; *Lasarte/Oria:* Martin Berasategui*; *Oiartzun/Oyarzun:* Zuberoa*, Matteo; *Zarautz/Zarauz:* Karlos Arguiñano.

VALENCIA
Alicante city: La Cantera, La Ereta, Monastrell, Nou Manolín. **Province:** *Cocentaina:* l'Escaleta; *Denia:* El Poblet, El Tossalet del Carme; *Dehesa de Campoamor:* Casa Alfonso; *Elche (Elx):* La Finca; *Moraira:* Girasol; *Petrer:* La Sirena; *Vila Joiosa:* El Emperador.
Castelló de la Plana city: Peñalén. **Province:** *Vinaròs:* El Faro de Vinaròs.
Valencia city: Ca'Sento, Rías Gallegas, La Sucursal, Torrijos.

Index

almonds
  almond and lemon-peel cake, Minorca-
    style 49
  chilled white almond soup Málaga-style 14
  egg, almond and sugar paste with a white
    chocolate crust and Malvasía ice 59
anchovies
  preserved north-coast anchovies 66
apple cream bun with apple sorbet and
    cider jelly 29
artichokes
  Tudela artichokes with chargrilled
    peppers and borage 164
asparagus
  white asparagus tempura with Roncal
    cheese mayonnaise 165

bacon
  almorta flour paste with bacon, garlic
    and paprika 88
  sweet chargrilled spring greens with
    bacon 64
beans and pulses
  chickpea stew with vegetables and
    assorted meats 145
  creamed kidney beans with blue-cheese
    fritters and spiced anchovy fillets 70
  white-bean stew with assorted pork cuts
    34
beef
  tender beef casserole with wild
    mushrooms, sweetened with vanilla 115
borrajas stems with rice and clams 26

cheese 23, 32, 37, 43, 62, 72, 118
  creamed kidney beans with blue-cheese
    fritters and spiced anchovy fillets 70
  goat's 52, 140, 150
  sheep's 72, 108, 140, 160, 165, 170
chicken stew, Chilindrón-style 27
cod
  deconstructed tomato, potato and
    vegetable 'omelette' with cod and
    beetroot 152
  salt cod with romesco sauce and fresh
    fruit 101

desserts
  almond and lemon-peel cake, Minorca-
    style 49
  apple cream bun with apple sorbet and
    cider jelly 29
  egg, almond and sugar paste with a white
    chocolate crust and Malvasía ice 59
  hot and cold hazelnut praline cake with
    chocolate and Elche dates 187
  lemon leaves deep-fried with eggs and
    cinnamon 158
  marzipan sponge with lemon verbena
    sorbet and liquorice crunch 91
  rice pudding Asturias-style with
    cinnamon ice cream and crunchy
    lemon 39
  sweet egg yolks with saffron cream and
    almond crust 79
  twenty-first century chocolate
    'breadcrumbs' 147
duck's liver
  roasted duck's liver on cherries with
    rose-scented almond cream 175
  terrine of ceps and duck's liver
    marinated in red wine 77

egg and onion fritters with tempura
    vegetables and a port and red-wine
    sauce 112
fish and seafood
  grilled fish with papaya cream and fresh
    coriander 54
  paella, Valencia-style 182
  pan-toasted black rice socarrat and baby
    octopus 100
  ravioli of octopus with confit potatoes
    in sweet paprika on a mussel cake 123
  traditional fish and seafood soup 178
  traditional rice stew with assorted meats
    or fish 44
gofio
  roasted corn, wheat and rye soup 58
hake
  fried hake on a bed of asparagus and
    green peppers 132
  hake Basque style with green peas,
    asparagus tips and parsley 176
  hake with cider sauce 36
ham
  fresh Mahón cheese with Iberian ham
    and dried tomatoes with olives and
    basil 47
  Idiazábal curd cheese with baby broad
    beans and Iberian ham 162
horse-mackerel
  spicy horse-mackerel stew with onion
    and baby squid 120

ice cream, cinnamon 39
kid
  marinated kid with new potatoes in a
    cider sauce 37
lamb
  lamb stew with bay leaves, garlic, hot
    pepper and white wine 76
  marinated rack of young lamb with
    rosemary, thyme and truffled bread
    cubes 135
  tender Aragón lamb shank with figs and
    mushrooms 24

meat
  chickpea stew with vegetables and
    assorted meats 145
  pan-fried bread cubes with an
    assortment of meats 89
  traditional rice stew with assorted meats
    or fish 44

octopus
  pan-toasted black rice socarrat and baby
    octopus 100
  ravioli of octopus with confit potatoes
    in sweet paprika on a mussel cake 123
omelette
  evolutionary Spanish omelette 144

paella, Valencia-style 182
partridge Toledo-style with glazed ceps and
    plums 86
pork
  black-pig pork fillet with a duo of Torta
    del Casar and vegetables 110

glazed suckling pig served on potato and
    almond nougat with lemon thyme 142
  Iberian charcuterie casserole with a
    sweet wine sauce 15
  sautéed borrajas with pork cheeks 136
  traditional stew, Galicia-style 125
  white-bean stew with assorted pork cuts 34
potatoes
  potatoes cooked Riojan style 130
  wrinkled potatoes with a spicy cumin
    sauce 56
prawns
  Dénia prawns with charcoal oil 184
  prawn kebabs with Majorcan sobrassada
    and mango salsa 48
  sweet Calasparra rice with king prawns
    and wine-scented cheese 157

rabbit with fresh rosemary 116
rice pudding Asturias-style with cinnamon
    ice cream and crunchy lemon 39

sardines
  crunchy smoked sardines with mixed
    vegetables 103
  sardine, tomato and red pepper pie 122
sausages 48
  round pork sausage with cabbage and
    potatoes 74
scorpionfish
  red scorpionfish cake 172
sea bream
  grilled sea bream with shellfish essence
    and peach confit 154
sea urchins with king prawns, rice and
    orange 185
soup
  borrajas stems with rice and clams 26
  chilled tomato soup with chopped egg
    and ham 12
  chilled white almond soup Málaga-style 14
  roasted corn, wheat and rye soup 58
  traditional fish and seafood soup 178
squid
  baby squid lasagne with truffle oil and
    avocado and spring onion salsa 167
  barbecued Basque squid with black rice
    and ceps 69
stews and casseroles
  chicken stew, Chilindrón-style 27
  chickpea stew with vegetables and
    assorted meats 145
  Iberian charcuterie casserole with a
    sweet wine sauce 15
  lamb stew with bay leaves, garlic, hot
    pepper and white wine 76
  tender beef casserole with wild
    mushrooms, sweetened with vanilla 115
  traditional rice stew with assorted meats
    or fish 44
  traditional stew, Galicia-style 125
  white-bean stew with assorted pork cuts 34
sturgeon
  deep-fried sturgeon with lime
    mayonnaise 17

tapas 17, 140
tomatoes
  chilled tomato soup with chopped egg
    and ham 12

vegetables, traditional roasted 98